THE ROUTE OF ALL EVIL

THE ROUTE OF ALL EVIL
The Political Economy of Ezra Pound

MEGHNAD DESAI

faber and faber

First published in 2006
by Faber and Faber Limited
3 Queen Square London WC1N 3AU

Typeset by Faber and Faber Limited
Printed in England by Mackays of Chatham plc,
Chatham, Kent

All rights reserved
© Meghnad Desai, 2006

The right of Meghnad Desai to be identified as author
of this work has been asserted in accordance with
the Copyright, Designs and Patents Act 1988

*This book is sold subject to the condition that it shall not,
by way of trade or otherwise, be lent, resold, hired out or
otherwise circulated without the publisher's prior consent in
any form of binding or cover other than that in which it
is published and without a similar condition including this
condition being imposed on the subsequent purchaser*

A CIP record for this book
is available from the British library

ISBN 978–0–571–21773–1
0–571–21773–7

2 4 6 8 10 9 7 5 3 1

Contents

Preface vii

I An Evil Genius or Just a Foolish One? 1

II The Mint Assayor's Son 24

III The Trouble With Money 46

IV Pound on Pound 77

V War and the Descent into Despair 117

VI Pound Foolish? 130

Select Bibliography 143

Index 149

Preface

The seed from which this book has sprung was planted in my mind nearly fifty years ago, when as a student in Bombay I came across one of the glossy American photo weeklies, either *Life* or *Post*. There was a feature on the poet as he was in St Elizabeth's, perhaps during his last few months there. The name stuck in my mind, and I looked him up in the card catalogue in the excellent library of the University of Bombay. Some time later, perhaps during the sixties, I picked up information about his radio broadcasts, and about his maverick views on money and usury.

There the idea lay for another thirty years or so, until I found time again in the summer of 2000, as I rummaged through my bookshelves, to pick up Nigel Stock's biography, which I must have bought in the downtown Manhattan second-hand bookshop, The Strand, on one of my many visits to New York. I found I had not only read it, but made notes about further reading on Pound's monetary ideas. So I began to think about writing an article, perhaps for some learned journal specializing in the history of economic ideas, about Pound's monetary heterodoxy.

One evening in the House of Lords in the Peers' Guest Room(the only bar where peers can entertain guests), the topic of Pound came up when my friends Matthew (Lord) Evans, formerly of Faber and Faber, and Robert (Lord) Skidelsky, the political economist and biographer of Keynes, joined me for a drink. It was then that Matthew Evans expressed the hope that Pound might yet make a comeback as an interesting author to read. I mentioned my curiosity about his economic ideas. I was encouraged to put up a proposal, and did so. I failed to deliver the manuscript as soon as I had hoped, but it did materialise by the summer of 2004. Here it is now, much improved by careful editorial and production inputs from my patient publishers.

I have many debts to acknowledge along the way. Lizzie Bacon was an efficient and cheerful colleague in the LSE Centre for the Study of Global Governance who used her mastery of English literature to trawl through the internet and provide an exhaustive reading list for me. The House of Lords Library is a treasure trove with the most capable and charming librarians, who scoured many libraries to obtain books and some rare pamphlets. I am indebted to them for their unfailing help. Robert Skidelsky and Matthew Evans provided much help by lending books and ideas. I was invited to give a plenary lecture at the Conference of the European Society for the History of Economic Thought in Venice on a rain-soaked evening in February 2004. I am grateful to Professor Cristina Marcuzzo for letting me try out my ideas on a stimulating audience.

My wife, Kishwar Desai, helped me to finish the first draft during Easter 2004 by taking over domestic chores. It was a doubly strange experience for her as we had just set up our home together, and she had to acclimatize herself to the lack of domestic staff in British life. I am deeply grateful to her for that and for much subsequent help. Dominique Enright was an efficient and careful editor who spotted the many small and a few large errors in the manuscript. I am indebted to her.

Perhaps I should also beg the indulgence of many Pound scholars and experts in English and American literature for bumbling into their territory. My inadequate effort will just show them how much better they could have done it.

Meghnad Desai
Venice/ Hastings/ London
November 2005

Abbreviations
of Ezra Pound's prose works
cited in this book

ABC	*ABC of Economics*
'America'	'America, Roosevelt and the Causes of the Present War'
'Bureaucracy'	'Bureaucracy the Flail of Jehovah'
'Economic Nature'	'An Introduction to the Economic Nature of the United States'
GW	*Gold and Work*
'Individual'	'The Individual in his Milieu'
'Money'	'What Is Money For?'
'Murder'	'Murder by Capital'
'Provincialism'	'Provincialism the Enemy'
PM	*Patria Mia*
'SC'	'Social Credit: An Impact'
'Shrine'	'The Jefferson–Adams Letters as a Shrine and a Monument'
SP	*Selected Prose 1909–1965*
VC	*A Visiting Card*

I
An Evil Genius or Just a Foolish One?

Ezra Pound was a fascist and an anti-Semite.

There it is. Let there be no doubt that this book is about a man who could be, and was, unpleasant.

Ezra Pound's fascism and anti-Semitism are not of a subtle kind. In the case of T. S. Eliot, his biographer Anthony Julius (*T. S. Eliot*, 1995) felt the need to argue passionately, but with a keen forensic intelligence, why that poet should be thought of as an anti-Semite. No such detective work is needed to make the same case against Pound. His sayings about Jews are transparent and frequent in his writings and speeches during the period he was settled in Rapallo, from 1924 until the end of the Second World War. Very much later in his life, he denied that he was either a fascist or an anti-Semite. He is even said to have recanted if not repented. But by then the damage had been done. Of course, his friends protest that he was kind to individual Jews – but then that is always said of racists or anti-Semites. Indeed, if you have to say such things, you already have conceded the point (see Reck, *Ezra Pound*, Chapter 5, pp. 122–31, and p. 146).[1]

Pound was also, however, a genius; a pioneer of modernism in English poetry; a generous helper of the likes of James Joyce, Ernest Hemingway and T. S. Eliot; a major poet of the twentieth century; a prolific prose writer; a lover of Japanese Noh theatre; an enthusiast for Chinese philosophy before many were ready to credit the Chinese with anything but sloth and superstition, and a musician of some note.

---

1 In what follows I shall take Pound's anti-Semitism as beyond doubt and not worth disputing. Julius (*T. S. Eliot*) has discussed it in some detail and gives references, see especially pp. 182–6.

Works of art, however fine, can as often be evil as benign. Leni Riefenstahl's powerful documentary film *Triumph of the Will*, for example, was superlative film-making and great propaganda for Hitler; just as D. W. Griffith's *The Birth of a Nation* is also a classic and beautiful film but one so racist in its views that it had a serious impact on American race relations. So it is with Pound's poetry, admired even though it is not free of his prejudices.

Ezra Pound, however, also wrote, spoke about and debated economic matters; he discussed money and credit, unemployment and working time, bankers and arms dealers. He felt that the Western civilization – which he cared deeply about – was being ruined because of the financiers' monopoly over credit, and argued that regaining control over credit was the key to solving the West's economic problems. He joined a long list of people who think they know the answer to all the misfortunes of the world, and in a time-honoured tradition of monetary radicals and cranks, he blamed bankers and Jews (treated as interchangeable categories) for their stranglehold on credit.

He was neither the first nor, alas, the last to spout such prejudices. After all, some form of anti-Semitism has been a part of European Christianity for two millennia. At times it seemed as if European Christians imbibed their anti-Semitism almost as casually as they imbibed their mother's milk. The hatred led to pogroms as well as daily harassment. It led many Jews to reject Judaism. It was fashionable in Germany in the early nineteenth century for Jews who thought themselves modern and who were ambitious, such as Karl Marx's father, to give up Judaism and convert to Christianity. Karl Marx's father did so, as did Felix Mendelssohn's – Abraham Mendelssohn even adding Bartholdy to his name to advertise his conversion. Marx himself wrote a complex and, some would say muddled, essay, *On the Jewish Question*, about how true liberation could arrive only when Jews ceased to be Jews.

AN EVIL GENIUS OR JUST A FOOLISH ONE?

But what for many centuries was just dull abuse of Jews, often emitted from pulpits, took on a more vicious aspect during the 1930s and was soon to have catastrophic effects. It is also in the 1930s and 1940s that Pound's anti-Semitism was on full display, and in the subsequent decades it was never totally disowned by him. For his acts of commission, especially his wartime radio broadcasts, and his failure to disavow crude prejudice, Ezra Pound is now reviled, whatever the quality of his poetry or the content of his economic and political ideas.

Yet Pound did not always hold bigoted, illiberal views. Indeed, his first forty-five years are very different from his last forty-two. He was a poet, a critic, a prolific promoter of schemes, a fund raiser for his friends in distress, a helpmate to all. From such commendable beginnings, he was to become a man reviled and demonized for his unpatriotic behaviour during the Second World War. The change was not just in the way people perceived him. He changed himself – and it is one task of my book to trace when and why this change happened. For happen it did and Ezra Pound is no longer just a great poet or a critic or a pioneer of modernism. He is the man who betrayed his country, who had to be incarcerated in a madhouse and who returned to his European exile once he was set free, unrepentant and unbowed.

It was clear to him early on during his college days that he was going to be a poet, but few expected him to be the force for modernism that he would become after his arrival in London in 1908 at the age of twenty-three. Indeed there are grounds for believing that Ezra Pound felt rejected by his native land. At the University of Pennsylvania he was unable to join a fraternity – a sure sign of non-acceptance by one's peers. He did not succeed in becoming a doctoral student or in retaining his job in a small college in Indiana. He had every reason to feel more at home in London, where he could play the brash outsider and display his talents. He emerged as a fertile generator of ideas, an incessantly active innovator, an encourager of talent, and an enthusiast for medieval French and Italian poetry. He became everyone's friend – including the elderly Henry James, W. B. Yeats ('Bill' to Pound) and the novelist Ford Madox Hueffer (who changed his German surname to 'Ford' during the First World War). Pound also promoted his college friend Hilda Doolittle in her career as the young poet H.D.; he was active in launching literary reviews and writing for other reviews; he translated Japanese Noh plays into English, and he championed Confucius and Mencius, learning Chinese in order to bring them to English readers. Along with Wyndham Lewis, another North American, he launched a revolution in the very style of conducting discourse about literature and art. He published fine slim volumes of poetry. He helped the young Tom Eliot with *The Waste Land* (to be rewarded with its dedication to *il miglior fabbro*), and trumpeted the merits of James Joyce.

Ezra Pound's dissatisfaction with the world in general, and with America in particular, starts with the reasonable complaint that in America, artists of merit did not find good employment. But it also came from a mixture of insecurity and bravado in his relationship with the land that had rejected him. Having left the United States in 1908 with a keen desire to win recognition for his talents, he returned there in 1911 for a brief period to see if a permanent return was suitable. His parents, especially his mother, were keen that he should take up a career – though he did say to her, 'Continued residence in America is of course most revolting to think of. But I might survive one winter and it might be useful perhaps' (Tytell, p. 55).

By this time he had already been compared to Robert Browning and hailed as one of the world's greatest poets by no less than Rudyard Kipling. Yet he remained unsure about the wisdom of going back. 'America presents itself to my mind as rather a horrible nightmare, a jaw of Tartarus effect ready to devour me if I lose grip on things present' (Tytell, p. 58).

Alas, America was not enthusiastic either. It did not devour him as he had feared. Rather, it spat him out. A permanent return was not feasible.

Two years after returning from his trip to America, he wrote in *Patria Mia*, 'The serious artist does not play up to the law of supply and demand' (*PM*, *SP*, p. 110). Americans, he felt, do not nourish their artists and writers: '[T]here is no man now living in America whose work is of the slightest interest to any serious artist' (*PM*, *SP*, p. 109). To him, if America did not want him, it was not worth living there in any case. After this trip of 1911, he did not return to his native land for twenty-eight years. *Patria Mia*, his commentary on American culture, is painfully aware of the provincialism of American culture as compared to that of France and England. Remember this is 1913 as yet and America is not what we see some ninety years on.

> America's position in the world of art and letters is, relatively, about that which Spain held in the time of the Senecas. So far as civilization is concerned America is the great rich Western province which has sent one or two notable artists to the Eastern capital. And that capital is, needless to say, not Rome, but the double city of London and Paris. (*PM*, *SP*, p. 114)

Provinces are everywhere liable to be dismissed by the metropolitan elite and London's elite had honed such dismissal to a fine art. Ezra Pound had now acquired this English talent. Four years later, in July 1917, three years into the First World War, in 'Provincialism the Enemy', published in the progressive magazine the *New Age*, Pound goes on to castigate Germany for its provincial nationalism and is relieved that his native country, though much influenced by Germany, has not fallen victim to such a narrow nationalism. But:

> England and France are civilization. They are civilization because they have not given way to the yelp of 'nationality' . . . More profoundly they have not given way to the yelp of 'race'

... This is modern civilization. Neither nation has been coercible into a Kultur; into a damnable Holy Roman Empire, holy Roman Church orthodoxy, obedience, Deutschland über Alles, infallibility Mousetrap. ('Provincialism', *SP*, p. 190)

The theme of Kultur as a hateful inhuman contrivance to be avoided is a theme which stays alive through the next twenty years. Yet the broad humanism implicit in the essay was slowly distorted into almost its opposite as Pound sank further into despair as a result of the war. Soon after coming to London, he had abandoned the Christian faith he had been brought up in. The Troubadours, whom he had studied, belonged to the heretical Cathar sect and were persecuted for it. With Yeats and Yeats's lover Olivia Shakespear (whose daughter, Dorothy, Pound was later to marry) he had experimented with the occult and dabbled in theosophy. The mystery cult of the Eleusinians with its celebration of sexuality was now his new religion. His attitude to Christianity became dismissive. 'The fundamental "philosophical" error or shortcoming is in Christianity itself,' he claimed. 'I think the world can dispense with the Christian religion, and certainly with all paid and banded together ministers of religion.'

The issue is intolerance which in turn leads to oppression: 'And Christianity has become the slogan of every oppression, of every iniquity' ('Provincialism', *SP*, p. 193). This is because of the desire of Christians to save the souls of others. 'Had He [Christ] possessed this faculty [of foresight] we might imagine His having dictated to His disciples some such text as "Thou shalt not 'save' thy neighbour's soul by any patent panacea or Kultur"' ('Provincialism', *SP*, p. 194).

Modernity is at this stage (during the First World War) the cry not just in literature but in life for Ezra Pound. He applauds 'the subtlest thinkers for the last thirty years', since they have thought about 'the means to prevent slavery to a "State" or a "democracy", or some such corporation...' He continues after some further discussion,

Modern thought is trying to kill not merely slavery but the desire to enslave; the desire to maintain an enslavement. This concept is a long way ahead of any actuality, it is a long way ahead of any working economic system that any of our contemporaries will be able to devise or to operate.
('Provincialism', *SP*, pp. 194–5)

The reference to an economic system – perhaps the first in Ezra Pound's writing – is as yet unspecific. His main concern is against oppression of any kind that stifles artists. But he is already searching for a better order. When he was flying the flag for modernism, he was confident that the enemy – the old-fashioned, the philistine, the provincial – would concede defeat quickly. Now there is a more combative feel to his writing because the world is more hostile and tougher. After nearly fifty years of peace, England was at war.

The First World War brought about a crisis in the literary world. When the Vortex group was launched by Pound and Lewis in the spring of 1914, with its own magazine *Blast*, they expected a rapid forward march towards the future, but once war started the world seemed to be going backwards, indulging in a feudal slaughter between the armies of competing aristocracies. The Vortex was chosen as a symbol of a fusion of artistic and sexual energy and advertised as such. The modernist shock of Vortex with its anti-Christian and anti-middle-class attitudes and explicit mention of testicles was met with repulsion and was rejected instead of being celebrated. The literary world had gone native and conservative. Bankers and arms salesmen were the most visible beneficiaries from this war-fuelled chauvinism. This was bad enough but in 1915 Pound's friend, and fellow Vorticist, the young and talented French sculptor Henri Gaudier-Brzeska had been killed in battle, which was to Pound an unbearable loss that he was still lamenting forty years later. There had to be deep roots to the social and economic crisis that followed closely on the heels of the war. Then, in 1919, another friend, A. R. Orage, editor of the *New Age*, met the engineer and economic theorist C. H. Douglas, a former major in the Royal Flying Corps, who claimed that he had the key to the crisis, an analysis of the problem of credit and its solution in the social control of credit. Pound became an instant convert to Douglas's concept of Social Credit.

A year later, Pound was launched on his new mission of explaining and propagating the theories of Social Credit and calling for the stranglehold of finance on the economy to be exposed. He moved from London to Paris in December 1920 and then in 1924 to Rapallo in Italy, away from where all the poets and artists were. It was his exile from exile. After the hostile reception Vortex had received, he had come to reject first England and then also France – the countries he had thought of as the high points of civilization when he first arrived on the European side of the Atlantic in 1908. He never contemplated going back to his native land – he had already rejected America. He had already begun his epic *Cantos* in London, during the war, and added to them in Paris; now, here in Dante's homeland, he pursued the twin tasks of economics and poetry.

But then something peculiar happened. He began to despair of any quick acceptance by the world of the truth of his messages, be it his *Blast* of modernism or of Douglas's solution for the world's economic problems. The despair first takes the form of pessimism about American culture of which he becomes more critical than he had been in his *Patria Mia*, which he wrote in 1911 and serialized in the *New Age* upon his return to London. He also demotes France from a civilized country, as he had described it in 1917, to one 'a weak nation, that having existed intellectually, and with most laudable activity, from 1830 onwards straight down to 1918 feels it has earned its rest. If it dies it will die at a respectable age' ('Bureaucracy', *SP*, p. 218).

This is in 1928, even before the Great Depression has hit; his vision gets darker as the Depression hits America and Europe. He sees more hope from Mussolini's speeches and action than from any American President.

> Mussolini is the first head of state in our time to perceive and to proclaim *quality* as a dimension in national production. He is the first man in power to publish any such recognition *since*, since whom? – since Sigismund Malatesta, since Cosimo, since what's-his-name, the Elector of Hanover or wherever it was, who was friendly with Leibniz? ('Murder', *SP*, p. 230)

England was now also no longer the other arm, with France, of civilization as it was in 1917. It had become the evil centre of financial power and had its stranglehold on America as well as much of Europe, except of course Italy and, later, Germany. Bankers, many of them Jews, were obstructing the return of prosperity by their monopoly of money and their usurious practices.

He re-evaluated the nature of what is good culture. Indeed the word culture or *kultur* is rejected in favour of the Greek word *Paideuma*.

> The term Paideuma has been resurrected in our time because of a need. The term Zeitgeist or Time Spirit might be taken to include passive attitudes and aptitudes of an era. The term Paideuma ... has been given the sense of the active element in the era, the complex of ideas which is in a given time germinal, reaching into the next epoch, but conditioning actively all the thought and action of its own time. ('For a New Paideuma', *SP*, p. 284)

Since England and France were no longer the places they had been, he located goodness in pre-Renaissance Italy. Good culture is now in a sense of gradations, a notion of hierarchy and order. 'A Mediterranean state of mind, state of intelligence, modus of order "arose" out of Sparta perhaps more than from Athens, it developed a system of gradations, an hierarchy of values among which was, perhaps above all other "order".'

By a sense of gradations he meant, as he explained, 'Things neither perfect, nor utterly wrong, but arranged in a cosmos, an order, stratified, having relations one with another' ('Shrine', *SP*, p. 150).

Now the decay of order is traced to the Renaissance, which for Pound is the beginning of the dark days of Europe:

> This Mediterranean paideuma fell before, or coincident with, the onslaught of brute disorder of taboo. The grossness of incult thought came into Europe simultaneously with the manifestations called 'renaissance', 'restoration' and muddled in our time with a good deal of newspaper yawp about puritans.
> ('Shrine', *SP*, p. 150)

There is a connection here with the decline in American culture. Pound began to dwell more on the early days of the Republic when Thomas Jefferson and John Adams were conducting their magnificent civilized correspondence. 'Jefferson's America was civilized while because its chief men were social. It is only in our gormy and squalid day that the chief of American powers have been, and are, anti-social' ('Shrine', *SP*, p. 150).

Ezra Pound's growing fascination with Jefferson relates back to Jefferson's contempt for banks and his insistence that the State need not issue any interest-bearing debt to finance its expenditure. Culture and economics come back together. As Pound's vision becomes less egalitarian and more anti-democratic, he prizes the elite of the early days of the Republic. He thinks Jefferson would have approved of Mussolini. Of course the consequence of forgetting the greatness of Jefferson and Adams and disregarding their fear of usury can be war. By 1937 Pound had reinterpreted the First World War:

> But Europe went blind into that war because mankind had not digested Jefferson's knowledge. They went into that war because the canon law had been buried, because all general knowledge had been split up into useless or incompetent frag-

ments. Because literature no longer bothered about the language 'of law and of the state' because the state and plutocracy cared less than a damn about letters. ('Shrine', *SP*, p. 153)

The war, which in 1917 he said was against provincialism of the German *kultur*, is now a folly of the usurers.

Pound wrote to senators and congressmen in the USA, but few took much note. He thought he could prevent the impending war; he had a cure for the world's ills – Social Credit reinforced by the stamp scheme of another European economist Silvio Gesell – so why wouldn't the world, America, FDR, listen? He returned to the USA in 1939, twenty-eight years since his last visit. He was fêted by his old college, but he noted bitterly how little Americans heeded his advice. The economics professors at Harvard had no time for him. In New York, he found too many Jews, even among his audience (Julius, p. 182). The despair turns then into bitter denunciation. His writing gets sharper, more directed at the evils, as he sees them, being perpetuated by England and America. He had been inveighing against religion, especially the monotheism of Christianity and by implication Judaism, even before the First World War. It all now comes together. A man who was a champion of humanism in 1917 is now bitterly on the side of fascism, thinking fully and consciously that it is superior to what is going on farther west.

So then, during the war, he agreed to broadcast on the Italian radio. He would not mouth Mussolini's propaganda but said he would give his personal views in order to educate those Americans who happened to be listening as to how sadly their country had gone wrong.[2] This was an error of judgement, especially after December 1941 when America entered the war.

2 Even Julius, who is sternly against all manifestations of anti-Semitism, observes (p. 183), 'Anti-Semitism saved Pound, as it saves others, from the efforts and disappointments of thought; "with one day's reading a man may have the keys in his hands," says Pound in Canto LXXIV. It is precisely this, however, that made his anti-Semitism so ineffectual. It lacked system, even elementary cogency.'

He should have known that this was an act which would be construed as treacherous if not treasonable. The public impact of his fascist broadcasts from Italy in wartime was small. He was not listened to by many, not as many as listened, for example, to Lord Haw-Haw (William Joyce), who was a major propaganda weapon for Hitler's war against the British. 'Most of [Pound's] short-wave broadcasts to America were so idiosyncratic they could hardly have corrupted the troops, even if he had wanted that' (Reck, p. 57). Had it not been that his native country was at war with the country where he by now had spent fifteen years of his life, his broadcasts would hardly have mattered. The world, after all, is full of cranks and some of them are geniuses. But there was a war on and Ezra Pound's fulminations on behalf of Mussolini were not looked upon kindly by the Americans.

He was indicted for treason *in absentia* in 1943. His friends among the literary fraternity worried about him: William Carlos Williams wondered if he would 'have the nerve to stand up and be shot if it comes to that'; Ernest Hemingway wrote to another friend: 'If Ezra has any sense he should shoot himself. Personally I think he should have shot himself somewhere along after the twelfth canto although maybe earlier.' (And yet the selfsame Hemingway was willing to go to the gallows in defence of his friend.) (Torrey, pp. 174–5.)

When the war ended in the defeat of the Fascist powers, he was arrested and hauled off to the USA to be indicted before an American court in Washington, DC.

A traitor he may have been, but he was nevertheless no ordinary traitor – in spite of his fascism there remained the fact that his greatest contribution was to modern poetry. The greatness of his verse far outweighed any impact his splenetic fascist outbursts may have had. So, fortunately for him, Pound was declared insane and not mentally fit to stand trial, incarcerated in a mental hospital for thirteen years and released only after a large international

AN EVIL GENIUS OR JUST A FOOLISH ONE?

appeal by many, including T. S. Eliot, Robert Frost, Archibald MacLeish. Thus he was never tried for treason and found either guilty or innocent. The charge was dismissed on the grounds that he would never be sane enough to stand trial.

Even so, Pound was lucky not to be sent to the electric chair. Only his rating as a genius and poet must have saved him. This, after all, was the man who was put in a cage in a prisoner-of-war camp constructed by the Americans in Italy for 'the most vicious or the most renegade' military prisoners. Half a square mile in area, it was ringed by a barbed-wire stockade, along which were sited fourteen guard towers. Pound was locked in a specially reinforced cage – ten feet square and seven feet high – and at night had to sleep on its concrete floor (Ackroyd, p. 86). Guantanamo Bay in more recent times is brought to mind.

As another of Pound's biographers reported,

> The night before Pound arrived, acetylene torches were seen as engineers reinforced one of the cages with heavy 'airstrip' steel, a fact which immediately caused the new prisoner to be held in awe: what manner of man was this who was so resourceful as to render insecure cells that had hitherto proved inviolable? But it was not fear of Pound breaking out, apparently, which led to these precautions, but fear that fascist commandos might break in and rescue him. (Stock, p. 408)

After three months, however, he was transferred to a hut inside a medical compound. He lived in a small tent and composed poems during the day and in the evening went to the dispensary where there was a typewriter. He managed to write eleven cantos – the *Pisan Cantos*, so called – which won him the newly instituted Bollingen-Library of Congress Award for Poetry in 1949.[3]

[3] This was a controversial decision and the Library of Congress which gave the prize was deprived of this privilege which passed on to Yale University. For Eliot's role in this award see Julius, pp. 205–8.

This book is not about Pound's poetry nor even about his fascism and anti-Semitism; not directly in any case. It is about his economics. Ezra Pound wrote more about economics in a sustained way than almost any other major creative writer in the English language in the twentieth century.[4] In his *Selected Prose*,[5] more than half of the 464 pages of text is taken up by his writings on economic matters. Indeed, after 1920, in virtually everything he wrote on – literature or religion or even obituaries of his friends – he could not avoid going off track about economics. For Pound economics was part of the solution to the problems of a proper funding for artists, of the quality of American culture, of the need to avoid hunger and poverty, of the need to ensure that high-quality craftsmanship of every kind gets its proper reward. His friend E. E. Cummings dreaded receiving a parcel from Pound fearing it would be yet another economics pamphlet.

Pound was obsessed with money and its influence on modern life. He was paranoid about usury and he said so in prose and poetry, bankers being his particular targets of hate. In his search for a neat solution to the economic ills of his times, especially in the interwar period, he was game for any scheme for reform – Major Douglas and his Social Credit, communism, fascism, Silvio Gessell and his stamp money notions, the agrarian radicalism of Thomas Jefferson, the bombastic rhetoric of Mussolini. He was for 'honest' money based on human labour, and he was against debt and bank credit, against the charging of interest on debt, and against gold and its stranglehold on money; and against the commodification of art, in particular the relatively low value put on it – as when a box of toilet rolls cost more than *La divina commedia* of Dante. (To be fair he was comparing the price of imported Ameri-

---

[4] Shaw is perhaps the only other writer I can think of – but he wrote on every social, economic and political topic.
[5] *Selected Prose 1909–1965*, ed. William Cookson, London: Faber, 1973; New York: New Directions Publishing Corporation, 1973.

can toilet rolls in Rapallo to an Italian printed copy of Dante's classic.) He was against twentieth-century capitalism, but for a sturdy agrarian capitalism of America in the pioneering days.

It is interesting to compare two views:

> Pound emerges [from 'bourgeois criticism'] as a canonized poet of major talent, worthy of practically endless study, but politically as a deluded crank or misguided liberal humanist, who can be on these grounds either dismissed or accommodated. (Brooker, p. 10)

> Pound's political commitments do not simply taint a greatness that nevertheless rises, phoenix like, above them. And they are, of course, to be condemned. But the politics of condemnation is in itself politically problematical. Pound's fascism and anti-semitism have their origins in a profound and potentially revolutionary dissatisfaction with the liberal settlement; the anticapitalist, antibourgeois fervour that motivates both need not have assumed the reactionary form it did. (Morrison, p. 4)

Of course both statements are true. Pound was a deluded crank. When charged with treason but sent for psychiatric examination, the doctors reported: 'He insists that his broadcasts were not treasonable, but that all his radio activities have stemmed from his self-appointed mission to "save the Constitution"' (Ackroyd, p. 91). Lest this be thought a plausible defence, look at this as a sample of a radio talk:

> I dislike quoting Jewish scripture. But the crop comes from the seed. By Jews you have betrayed a number of nations. And by the Jews you will, I think, in your turn be betrayed . . . the kike is all out for power. The kike and the unmitigated evil that is centred on London . . . And every sane act you commit is committed in homage to Mussolini and Hitler . . . (Ackroyd, p. 85)

But the same deluded crank also wrote this:

> The error has been *pecuniolatry*, or the making of money into a god. This was due to a process of denaturalization, by which our money has been given false attributes and powers that it should never have possessed.
>
> Gold is durable, but does not reproduce itself – not even if you put two bits of it together, one shaped like a cock, the other like a hen. It is absurd to speak of it as bearing fruit or yielding interest. Gold does not germinate like grain. To represent gold as doing this is to represent it falsely. It is falsification.
>
> The stamp affixed to the note acts as the hair-spring in the watch. Under the usurocratic system the world has suffered from alternate waves of inflation and deflation, of too much money and too little. Everyone can understand the function of a pendulum or hair-spring. A similar mental grasp should be brought to bear in the field of money.
>
> A sound economic system will be attained when money has neither too much nor too little potential. The distinction between trade and usury has been lost. The distinction between debt and interest bearing debt has been lost.
> (*GW*, p. 14)

Read him like this and Ezra Pound is a contemporary marching against Third World debt or against globalization along with the thousands in Genoa, Seattle, Porto Allegre and Florence. Or he is one with the universal and age-old concern with debt and usury, which existed in medieval Christianity as in present-day Islam. His anti-capitalism is of an unusual kind. As an American born on the Wild West frontier in Idaho with a grandfather who felled timber forests in Wisconsin and printed his own money and a father who was an assayer of the Mint in Philadelphia, Ezra Pound was a red-blooded supporter of free enterprise. As one critic put it,

In *Patria Mia*, for example, he had spoken of 'the type of man who can hold on to the profits of subsequent industry . . . a close person, acquisitive, rapacious, tenacious'. In contrast, he defined the 'serious artist' as one who 'must be as open as nature' and this preference for mobility and 'energy' were related, obliquely but suggestively, to what he saw as the positive side of American capitalism: 'I do not say that the American is wholly without sense of property, but his sense of play and of acquisition are [sic] much keener than his sense of retention.' (Nicholls, p. 25)

Ezra Pound is thus at the same time a fascist and an anti-Semite but also a protester against modern capitalism in its obsession with monetary calculus, commodification and indeed devaluation of artistic enterprise. He dislikes bankers intensely and attributes to usury many of the ills of modern times. Even after the Second World War and his incarceration, he carried on his polemic about money and banking, about the possibility of re-establishing a yeoman capitalism of the kind on which America was based in the days of Jefferson and Adams. In these days of Jubilee 2000 and the Global Justice movement, and of calls to build capitalism on a local basis as Walden Bello and others have argued for, Pound is your man.[6]

In the following chapters I want to explore Pound's ideas on economics, both for what they were in the context of what economics was like in his own days and also for their relevance for us today. This is because Ezra Pound, poetical genius that he was, was also one in a long tradition of money cranks whose ideas are unorthodox and troubling but yet contain a germ of radical thinking about the economic order. America has a rich heritage of such money cranks ever since the Pilgrim Fathers landed on its shores, and that

---

[6] For details on the different perspectives in the anti-globalisation movement see Said and Desai (2003) in Kaldor, Anheier and Glasius, *Global Civil Society Yearbook 2003*.

tradition is still alive today.[7] There is also in America a fascinating history of experiments with money in various territories and regions both before and after 1776 (Lester, 1939/1970). There was a sturdy battle between commercial and financial capitalism, emerging just as America became independent, and the Augustan ambience of agrarian capitalism. It was Jefferson against Hamilton. Later still, Andrew Jackson fought a battle against Nicholas Biddle and his bank, a battle that continued in various guises under his successor Martin Van Buren. After the Civil War, there is a battle against Resumption – a return to the Gold Standard – and for inflation by printing more greenbacks or adopting silver coinage. The battle lasts up to 1896, with William Jennings Bryan's candidature for Presidency and his defeat. This was the first election Pound was old enough to follow with interest. The East Coast where he was growing up was all for gold while the West and the South-West were all for Bryan. So the seeds of monetary radicalism could have been laid then.

But there is also a lively debate in Britain from the seventeenth century onwards wherein people have expressed violently contrasting views on the true nature of money and the right cure for the ills it causes (Corry, 1962). There was a suspicion of public debt which allowed the Walpole ministry in the early eighteenth century to borrow money to fight wars rather than to resort to Parliament for additional taxation for each war. The battle in the late nineteenth century and later was often between finance and industry, and political leaders across generations – Disraeli and Churchill among them – were for checking the power of bankers. In the 1970s politicians became convinced that a control over money would cure all our ills and introduced monetarism – with the result that millions had to endure unemployment and misery (Desai, 1981). Nowadays there are lively controversies on the Euro,

7 A recent example is Zarlenga, Stephen, *The Lost Science of Money: The Mythology of Money – the Story of Power*, 2002.

on Third World Debt and the evil doings of the International Monetary Fund, of speculative bubbles on the foreign exchange markets which transact a trillion-plus dollars a day. There are schemes to tax the foreign exchange (forex) transactions such as the Tobin Tax, originally proposed by the Nobel Prize-winning American economist James Tobin (who, however, later faced with its adoption on the wilder shores of the anti-globalization movement, disowned it). Others have proposed that the IMF be replaced by a proper global bank which will issue cheap credit to the world's poor, thus reviving a proposal Keynes made during the discussions which led up to the Bretton Woods Conference in 1944.[8] Ezra Pound would have felt quite at home in this climate.

But a critique of capitalism can extend beyond mere economics. It can, as with William Morris and John Ruskin, dwell on the quality of life, the beauty of products made by hand rather than by machine. It can be a protest against the commodification of art and spirituality. It can, as Shaw did in *Heartbreak House*, blame war and mass deaths on the profit motive of armament manufacturers. Ezra Pound's journey to an economic critique starts with a critique of culture, which in its then distorted form he labels *Kultur*. It is only later that this *Kulturkampf* develops into a total critique of modern capitalism with the paradox that the humanistic champion of modernism in art becomes an implacable enemy of any humanistic influences on the grounds that since his favourite economic panacea is not adopted by the Allies, they have forfeited the claim to any humane treatment. The issue is no longer just culture or language but the desirability of the economic order under which he had lived for so long. Yet in many ways his economic policy proposals are very radical – full employment with short working hours, interest-free debt, a national dividend or what we would today label citizens' income. The puzzle is that in advocating what

8 Monbiot (2003); for Keynes's original proposal and the background for it, see Skidelsky (2003).

is not by any means undesirable or even unfeasible, he managed to make himself into an enemy of his nation.

It is also, however, worth exploring whether his economic radicalism or even monetary crankiness had to be mixed up with his virulent anti-Semitism. This is not to excuse but to understand the nature of the disease that his anti-Semitism became. For each strand of Pound's economic thinking, one can cite other writers who share the thought but are immune from the disease. The despair and the bitterness which grow after his self-imposed exile to Rapallo draw as much upon the sense of rejection of the diasporic genius as of the young student who could not win admission to fraternities on his campus. They feed on the notion of the expatriate that 'home' is not what it used to be – that it has been taken over by the new arrivals, the scum of central Europe who have been pouring across the Atlantic on to the streets of New York and other East Coast cities. The huddled masses appear in a troublesome way in *Patria Mia* already. They may be anonymous and amorphous in 1911 but by 1939 they become all Jews in Pound's imagination.

Early on in *Patria Mia*, Pound writes, 'People marvel that foreigners deluge America and "lose their own nationality almost at once"; that "their children all look alike".' He goes on:

> It must be considered that the men who come to America from Hungary, or from Sweden, Kravats, Slavs, Czechs, Italians, Germans, are men of similar tastes and of similar intentions. Irish or Russian Jew, the man comes with the determination to improve his material condition.
>
> We get from every village the most ruthless and the most energetic. The merely discontented stop in England. We get the 'materialist' and the 'idealist'. I use both these words with irony. The idealist who comes to us is a man with a belief in the future, especially his own future. He knows what he wants. He wants to be better off.

> The other 'idealist', the non-constructive idealist, the person who is content with his own thoughts, the person whom it is the fashion to call 'sentimentalist', does not emigrate. I mean the person who has 'the finer feelings', love of home, love of land, love of place, of atmosphere, be he peasant or no. He may come as an act of heroism, but he returns to his land. He is almost negligible in our calculations. He has instinct; he is not 'idealist', for this reason, namely, that no cliché, no catchword, no set of phrases will induce him to forget the marrow of life as he in his unanalysed heart knows it to be.
> (*PM, SP*, pp. 101–2)

Apart from the (as yet positive) awareness of the foreigner, there is a telling self-indictment here of the exile who has decided not to return. If Pound had emigrated to England 'as an act of heroism', he was not now contemplating a return to his native land. And yet we see that it is with this person who 'in his unanalysed heart' cannot forget the marrow of life that Pound sympathises. Pound then goes on in this piece to hope that America will have its Renaissance – not yet the dirty word it was to become within a decade. It is almost as if he is making an offer to America: have a Renaissance, value your artists and writers properly, and I will return. 'America,' he goes on, 'has a chance for Renaissance and that certain absurdities in the manners of American action are, after all, things of the surface and not of necessity the symptoms of sterility or even of fatal disease.'

Yet the foreigners may be a problem.

> One returns from Europe and one takes note of the size and vigour of the new strange people. They are not Anglo-Saxon; their gods are not the gods whom one was reared to reverence. And one wonders what they have to do with lyric measures and the nature of 'quantity' . . .
> One knows they are the dominant people and that they are

against all delicate things. They will never imagine beautiful plaisaunces. They will never 'sit on a midden and dream stars' ... (*PM, SP*, p. 104)

So, long before the First World War and Douglas, Pound had seen that the barbarians were not only at the gate but right inside and had become the dominant people. Above all they were incapable of plaisaunces. The cultural pessimism went deeper as the years passed by and the exile who refused to return only got tied up with finance and *Götterdämmerung* when the penny dropped that these barbarians could belong to the same religion as the bankers who were the root of the problem. No wonder that when he went back in 1939 for what he thought was his last chance to save America from joining a European war, Pound was upset that among the fans who had come to hear him in New York there were, according to him, 'too many Jews'.

There may thus be an explanation for his anti-Semitism which can be distanced from his economic radicalism. On a rereading of his early prose, his anti-Semitism can be seen to be deeply rooted in a feeling of alienation from his native land. And yet even while he lived there during his first twenty-three years, Pound was not entirely at home. He was an outcast since he was never accepted as 'one of us' by his fellow students and indeed behaved in a sufficiently eccentric manner to deserve their puzzlement (Torrey, pp. 24-30). This awkwardness became a mark of genius when he hit London and so he perfected it and indeed in Paris and later Rapallo he became a victim of the persona he had created for himself.

His economic radicalism comes from quite different sources – from his despair at the rejection of Vorticism, the tragedy of the war and the death of Gaudier-Brzeska. But even then, for fifteen years after the end of the war, this economic radicalism remains dormant. It is when the Depression hits Europe, and indeed America, that Pound begins to get insistent and impatient about Social Credit. Unfortunately, his hatred for bankers and armament manufacturers and dealers (such as Sir Basil Zaharoff), dating from the First World War, mixes in with his monetary radicalism.

There is as well a paradox here: during the late nineteenth and early twentieth centuries in both Europe and America, Jews were excluded from many occupations open to gentiles. So they congregated in certain occupations, not by choice but because there was little option – and these occupations happened to be in finance and commerce, journalism and cultural activities. At the same time, many Jews drifted to the Communist Party which made them feel welcome, or other radical causes whose adherents were more cosmopolitan. As chance had it, these were the fields of activity that Pound blamed for all the world's ills, banking and finance especially. The climate in Italy and Germany fed this hatred further, while his despair about America turned into a hatred for Roosevelt (a sentiment which was widely shared in America itself during the thirties), which coincided with his discovery of Jefferson and his fancy that somehow Mussolini was the Jefferson of his times. This cocktail of personal and political opinions turned lethal when the Second World War broke out, with what are now known to be extremely damaging consequences for Pound's reputation.

II
The Mint Assayor's Son

Ezra Pound has been well served by biographers so I shall only give here the barest details.[1] He was born in Hailey, Idaho on 30 October 1885, son of Homer Loomis and Isabel Weston Pound. Ezra's grandfather, Thaddeus, had been involved in the timber trade in Northern Wisconsin and rose to be a Senator; he actually issued his own scrip to pay his workers, which they could use as money. Homer, who did not quite achieve the status his father had enjoyed, was a Registrar of Land Claims in Idaho, which was frontier country and as yet only recently settled, but the family soon moved to Philadelphia where he became an Assistant Assayor of the US Mint. Ezra studied at the University of Pennsylvania and then Hamilton College in upstate New York. After a brief spell at Wabash College in Indiana as an instructor, he left for Europe in 1908 and soon settled in London. He was by then publishing poetry and experimenting with modern forms as well as studying French troubadour poetry and befriending writers and artists, many of them American exiles like himself in London.

The America Pound left was very different from the one we know today. It was sparsely settled except on the East Coast, and the thirty years between 1885 and 1914 were the years of mass migration from Europe to America. There was also a simultaneous process of industrial growth and agricultural depression. Prices of foodstuffs were falling across the world as a result of the discovery of new sources of supply as well as the revolution in transport. American farmers had enjoyed high prices during the Civil War and contracted debts. But after the Civil War, America

1 I have used Stock (1970), Kenner (1975), Reck (1968), Torrey (1984), Tytell (1987) plus other sources which will be cited in appropriate places.

went through a period of monetary consolidation and adopted the Gold Standard. This led to a squeeze on all the debtors, with prices falling and interest rates high. There was a strong political movement for silver to supplement gold as the basis of currency and William Jennings Bryan as the Presidential candidate of the Democratic Party ran three times on an anti-gold ticket. The demand for silver was a demand for easy money, which is what the debtor farmers and the industrialists wanted. The 'Robber Barons' – a mixed category consisting of railroad tycoons, oil men, trust manipulators and bankers – were sound money men who identified with the Republican Party and lived on the East Coast. They were painted as the enemy of the farmers. The bankers were aware, as were some of the leaders in big business, that the United States had to rely on European capital to expand and to build railroads, telephones and factories. They wanted sound money to guarantee a steady flow of this foreign capital. The people in the interior wanted easy money and high prices for their produce. The silver movement and the anti-banking mood became stronger the farther west and south you went.

Ezra Pound grew up on the East Coast and here there was a clear distinction between old settled Americans such as his family and the new arrivals. Of course while his father had a respectable job, as son of a Senator, Homer Pound was an example of gentle decline in the economic pecking order. On his mother's side, the Westons were richer and more willing to spoil Ezra than his father could afford to. It was with his great-aunt Frances (Frank) Weston that he first visited Europe in the summer of 1898. This was America's Gilded Age. The East Coast thought of itself very much as an extension of Europe, especially England, and travel to Europe was very much part of the well-heeled young man's education, rather like the Grand Tour for the sons of the English aristocracy in the eighteenth century. There was also at the same time a feeling of cultural inferiority relative to Europe, a cultural cringe which is well reflected in Pound's *Patria Mia*.[2]

Pound attended the University of Pennsylvania, the oldest university (Harvard is the oldest college) in North America, but only for two years. He was unhappy there and was excluded from the social life of the fraternities. He moved to Hamilton College in upstate New York. After some graduate work back at Penn he secured a job at Wabash College in Indiana but was sacked because he offended the locals by sheltering an itinerant actress in his apartment. America was not for him and off he went to Europe at the age of twenty-three.

Internationally, the half-century before the First World War was an age of globalization. There was free movement of money under the Gold Standard and free movement of capital and labour. The Bank of England was effectively the central bank for the world as it manipulated its bank rate to keep the British pound freely convertible into gold. Money could be sent anywhere without worry about exchange rates. Passports were not necessary for travellers within the North Atlantic region. Britain and France ruled large empires across the globe and London and Paris were global cities. For the well-to-do of Western Europe, this was the Belle Époque.

This was also a period of ideological ferment. Socialism was emerging as an important force with the inauguration of the Socialist International in Paris in 1889. Anarchists, syndicalists, guild socialists and Christian socialists were all vying for attention within the socialist movement. There was also an upsurge of nationalism especially in eastern and south-eastern Europe and parts of Asia. Many of these movements made their homes in Paris and London. Pound does not seem to have taken any interest in

---

2 The best way to convey a feel for America at that time is to compare it to Australia as it was in the 1970s and 1980s when there was the same sense of cultural inferiority vis-à-vis England, which was hotly debated in the magazines and newspapers as I well remember from my visits in 1980 and 1984.

political or social movements in London, where there was much else to occupy his interests. It was an exciting time in the arts, with the Impressionists being succeeded by the Cubists, while Dada and the Futurists were shocking the world. Meanwhile, there was a lot of cross-fertilization among the literatures of different languages: Rabindranath Tagore had come to London with his Bengali poetry, which caught the attention of Yeats and Pound, and there was a growing awareness of the Chinese and Japanese languages.

Pound joined in this revolutionary ferment of the artistic world with gusto, paying scant attention to the political world. He enjoyed shocking people and 'scandalized many by wearing one ear-ring, startling others by springing to his feet and bowing stiffly' (Judd, p. 166). At other times...

> With green trousers made of billiard cloth, with his pink velvet coat and its blue glass buttons, a hand-painted tie, his mane of reddish blond hair tucked under a sombrero, his green eyes, a beard cut to a point to resemble a Spanish conquistador, and as a final touch a singular turquoise earring, Pound strode the London streets as operatically as any character of Puccini's. (Stock, p. 225)

Some years later, Sir Herbert Read wrote, 'Apart from his exotic appearance, he rattled off his elliptic sentences with a harsh nasal twang, twitched incessantly, and prowled round the room like a caged panther. He was not made for compromise or co-operation, two qualities essential for any literary or artistic "movement"' (Tytell, p. 5).

It was here that he met Henry James, Ford Madox Hueffer (Ford) and W. B. Yeats. He published his own poetry steadily in these years – *A Lume Spento* (1908), *Personae* (1909), *Exultations* (1911), as well as his lectures, *The Spirit of Romance*, in 1910. He travelled extensively in France, Italy and Germany during 1911 and brought back troubadour poetry from France which he translated. He launched his Imagist movement soon after and then met Wyndham Lewis with whom he instigated the Vorticist movement. Wyndham Lewis called Pound the Trotsky of literature and added that he was 'a demon pantechnicon driver, busy with the removal of old world into new quarters' (Materer, pp. 32).

He married Dorothy Shakespear in 1914. Her mother Olivia was a friend and former lover of W. B. Yeats and a writer herself. Dorothy was enchanted by Ezra Pound on their first meeting:

> He has a wonderful, beautiful face, a high forehead, prominent over the eyes; a long delicate nose, with little red nostrils; a strange mouth, never still, & quite elusive; a square chin, slightly cleft in the middle – the whole face pale; the eyes grey-blue; the hair golden brown, and curling in soft wavy crinkles. Large hands, with long, well-shaped fingers and beautiful nails.
> (Tytell, p. 45)

This is indeed a woman in love. Within five years of this, they were married. The marriage tied Pound even closer to England and drew him away from America.

It is not clear when Pound became interested in economic and political questions. One source says that it was through his friendship with Ford Madox Ford. Ford brought out a magazine called the *English Review* in 1908 and its first issue contained an article by a Cambridge mathematician, Arthur Marwood, called 'A Complete Actuarial Scheme for Insuring John Doe against all the Vicissitudes of Life'. The scheme in question anticipated much of the welfare state which was being launched at about the same time through Lloyd George's measures. Ford's biographer says that it was this article 'which may have influenced Pound in his unfortunate enthusiasm for economics'. (Judd, p. 166)

More frequently it is suggested that A. R. Orage, whom he met in 1911, inspired him to take an interest in social and economic questions. Orage (1873–1934) is one of those unusual figures who are extremely influential in the lives of people who become more famous than themselves, but cannot be brought alive in print later. Orage was born of poor parents and with the help of a Sunday school teacher managed to finish his school education. He then trained as a teacher in Leeds but became a socialist upon hearing the trade union leader Tom Mann. He was active in the Leeds branch of the Independent Labour Party and wrote a literary column for Keir Hardie's weekly, the *Labour Leader*. But Orage was ideologically promiscuous. He dabbled in Plato and Nietzsche, lectured on Gurdjieff and was influenced by the *Bhagavadgita* and the *Mahabharata*. He came to London in 1907 and with some help from Bernard Shaw started the *New Age* which spread the word for Socialism not merely of the Fabian variety but also Guild Socialism and of course Social Credit.[3]

But Orage also cared about the autonomy of literature and considered language as a repository of value and medium of cultural exchange. This intimate connection between language as a medium of exchange, and money as a similar medium in social exchange is one that Pound picked up and developed. Pound was invited to write regularly for the *New Age*; indeed for some months what Orage managed to pay him was his principal means of support, supplemented by what Homer Pound could send him occasionally.

The war shocked many of Orage's contemporaries. Socialists had thought that they could bring an end to the warring habits of capitalism by combining across the many nations in a workers' solidarity movement. Rationalists like Bertrand Russell and Bernard Shaw could not comprehend the slaughter. Much of the previous century had been seen as a march of Reason and Progress. Indeed, Pound and Wyndham Lewis were impatient to move the world into new quarters, as Wyndham Lewis put it. Yet

3 For Orage's life see Wallace Martin (ed.), *Orage as Critic*, Introduction, pp. 1–16.

here was carnage and a throwback to feudal rivalries. Lewis wrote later, 'We are the first men of a Future that has not materialized. We belong to a "great age" that has not "come off".'[4]

For Pound there was also a personal shock. Henri Gaudier-Brzeska, a young and talented sculptor, became a close friend of Pound in London. They had met at the Albert Hall in 1913 where Gaudier-Brzeska – who had a studio under a railway bridge in Putney (to which Pound alludes many times in his subsequent writings) – was exhibiting his works. They became friends and Gaudier-Brzeska sculpted a large head of Pound, who supplied the marble. Gaudier-Brzeska joined the war as a French citizen and it was through his account of trench warfare that Pound became personally touched by the war. Then in June 1917, Henri Gaudier-Brzeska died in action. His 'manifesto', written while he was in the trenches, was published in *Blast*: 'This war is a great remedy. In the individual it kills arrogance, self-esteem, pride. It takes away from the masses numbers of unimportant units, whose economic activities become noxious as the recent trade crises have shown us' (Stock, p. 182).

The sense of loss of a Future became much more real with Gaudier-Brzeska's death. Pound told Wyndham Lewis that his 'serious curiosity' about politics and economics began at Gaudier-Brzeska's death. Pound was still grieving for him when Charles Olson met him in St Elizabeth's in the late 1940s.[5] It was about this time, during the First World War that Orage met Major Clifford Hugh Douglas who had his own radical views of how to cure trade crises and prevent the wastage of human lives. This combination of a personal loss and a perceived miracle cure provided the catalyst that drove Pound into a lifelong involvement with economics.

---

4 Wyndham Lewis, *Blasting and Bombardiering*, p. 258 quoted by Materer, 1979, p. 61.
5 Materer, p. 67, citing EP's letter to WL, 25 January 1949. Charles Olson and EP: *An Encounter at St. Elizabeth's*, ed. Catherine Sayle, p. 45.

The time was also ripe for it. The years before the war had their ups and downs, their trade cycles and crises, but on the whole Western Europe and North America had emerged as prosperous developed countries. Prices had been steady or falling and wages had risen even in the USA despite the large influx of immigrants. The Gold Standard had made all money freely convertible at a fixed rate; the pound sterling, for example, standing at $4.86. Now, that steady pace of economic life had been disrupted. There had been full employment through the war and trade unions had been recognized as powerful social forces to be harnessed for the war. But in 1917 the Russian Revolution occurred, and soon after Germany, defeated and exhausted, became a republic. There were socialist rebellions in Hungary, Austria, Germany and Northern Italy.

There was also inflation at the rate of twenty per cent-plus in the immediate aftermath of the war. The years of 1919 and 1920 saw post-war dislocation in economic activity in the loser countries, and booms and shortages in the victor countries. Inflation continued apace in Austria and Germany during the early twenties and became, in the words of a later historian, the 'Great Disorder' (Feldman, 1993). The impoverishment of German middle classes is blamed on the hyper-inflation of 1923 and 1924, which in Britain was brought under control with a savage cut in public expenditure with the so-called Geddes Axe (after the ex-MP who was asked by the Treasury to propose ways of balancing the Budget). Germany had to be rescued by an American-led international plan which restored its currency's value. But the hurt and damage inflicted by the reparations payments imposed by the Treaty of Versailles, and the hyperinflation lasted a much longer time in Germany.

The Gold Standard had been suspended by many of the belligerent nations and currency fluctuations added to the overall uncertainty. There were now barriers to the free movement of people; for an alien American like Ezra Pound, passports and visas became essential even to go from London to Paris. He had to confront bureaucrats to get his permission to travel. It was the end of the Belle Époque.

There was something clearly wrong with the world and a search was on for what it was. Many in the Establishment were impatient for a return to normality, to the Gold Standard, to the liberal economic order of pre-war days. Others sought a revolutionary change.

The connection between trade crises which caused unemployment and misery, and war as their cure detected by Gaudier-Brzeska was analysed by Lenin in his *Imperialism* pamphlet. But it was also familiar even before the war to many other socialists.[6] But could there not be a way of running the economy which would avoid the crises and also not require the slaughter caused by war?

Orthodox economics at that time did not admit that such a question was even worth asking. Its belief in a liberal laissez-faire order was so strong that economists to a man (and they were all men) believed that the crisis was transitory. As soon as wartime expenditure was reduced and public debt paid off, the economists argued, the markets would start functioning properly again and full employment would be restored (although the term 'full employment' had as yet not been invented). The Marxists thought that capitalism was a busted flush and that only a revolution could solve the problem. In between, there were various concerned groups which were floundering around for an answer. Socialists of various hues – Christian, syndicalist, Guild – were unhappy with the situation and thought some change was necessary. There was also a general feeling of decay and crisis in Europe as such. There were books warning of a terminal crisis of the civilization. Oswald Spengler's *Decline of the West* and Sidney and Beatrice Webb's *The Decay of Capitalist Civilisation* are but two examples of this genre.

---

6 I have discussed the connection between war, capitalism and imperialism in my *Marx's Revenge*, Chapters 6–8.

It was in this context that Major Douglas came up with his answer to the economic question. It was the control of credit, or Social Credit as he called it. I shall come to his answer in some detail in a subsequent chapter. But his advocacy of Social Credit as a panacea appealed to Ezra Pound. Here at last was a connection between unemployment and trade crises, and a solution. Douglas was not an economist but an engineer – a practical sort of chap, not an academic theorist. He had built aircraft and the underground railway in London for the Post Office. He had worked in India. If he said he had the answer and demonstrated it in a short book, *Economic Democracy*, what more could one ask?

Ezra Pound reviewed *Economic Democracy* for the *Athenaeum* and also for the *Little Review*. These were his first writings on economics. Their tone is anti-corporatist, anti-totalitarian, anti-Fabian. The basic message is clear as Pound praises 'his perception, very clear and hard headed, that the ultimate control of industry is financial control' ('Probari Ratio', *SP*, p. 207). The theme of financial control by the state rather than by private creditors – the banks – thereafter becomes a constant theme in Pound's writing.

Economic Democracy came out in 1920 and it was at the end of this year that Pound moved to Paris. He had been unhappy in London since the beginning of the war. The Vorticist movement and its magazine *Blast* had shocked many people by its explicit scatological and sexual references. The war made people conservative and simplemindedly patriotic. Modernism was no longer an urgent issue. Pound's hectoring style was also beginning to grate on his friends and even his protégés such as Robert Frost. He was short of money and a move to Paris seemed to promise something better. The *New York Herald* reported that he had said that 'His reason [for leaving London] is that he finds "the decay of the British Empire too depressing a spectacle to witness at close range".' He also told the newspaper that 'he can see no economic improvement without revision of the credit system'. His plans for his stay in France were to study twelfth-century music and write a long poem (Stock, pp. 235–6). This was very much what he did while in France and apart from short reviews of Douglas's books as they came out he did not write any economics in France.

But then in 1924 he moved to Rapallo. This is a puzzling move. Obviously he was always short of money and living would be cheaper in a small town in Italy than in London or Paris. He had visited Venice when he first left his native land in 1908 and liked it very much. Rapallo is not Venice; far from it – it is a small Italian town on the opposite coast, a holiday resort on the Italian Riviera and the site of the signing of three treaties during and after the First World War. Max Beerbohm – the Jew 'Brennbaum' in Pound's poem *Hugh Selwyn Mauberly* – also lived there. This move isolated Pound further. It was a rejection of his old connections, a withdrawal from England and France, his two major loves with whom he had now fallen out. But as a biographer of Ford Madox Ford has written, this may have affected his mental make-up.

> Pound may have developed as he did partly as a result of cutting himself off. He did it in various ways but Rapallo represented the geographical, which is important because it removed him from regular converse with friends such as Ford – perhaps even uniquely with Ford – with whom he could disagree without falling out, who could tease him, who could pat him on the shoulder and remind him that they went back a long way, who could at the same time as accepting him, provide the conflict with other minds without which many good minds are lost. (Judd, p. 368)

Whether there were deeper reasons behind his decision to cut himself off as he did is an open question. He was about to be forty, which can be a critical age for men and women; he was of course interested in Italian literature, in Dante and Malatesta. He does not seem at this stage to have noticed Mussolini much. But his isolation both geographical and intellectual was to cost him dear. He was no longer subject to the critical attention of Orage or Ford or Wyndham Lewis or Eliot. He seems not to have given any thought to a return to his native land. The exile continued. It only became truly acute now that he was away from what he had called the double capital of civilization, Paris and London. He was to plough a lonely furrow.

He began to take an interest in the Russian Revolution and wrote for the American Communist periodical *New Masses*. But soon he also became fascinated by what Mussolini was doing. As he liked Mussolini more, he began to dislike American politicians in the same proportion.

'I personally think extremely well of Mussolini,' he wrote to Harriet Monroe, the editor of *Poetry* magazine and a long-time correspondent, two years after arriving in Rapallo, 'with whom it is impossible to compare the last three American Presidents or British Prime Ministers without insulting him' (Stock, p. 265). One of his reasons for liking Italy, indeed Europe in general, and not liking America was the economic prospect for artists.

A short note on 'The State', which came out in his new journal, *The Exile*, in spring 1927 is the first published indication of his new mood.

> Both Fascio and the Russian revolution are interesting phenomena; beyond which there is the historic perspective.
> ... The capitalist imperialist state must be judged not only in comparison with unrealized utopias, but with past forms of the state; if it will not bear comparison with the feudal order; with the small city states both republican and despotic; either as to its 'social justice' or as to its permanent products, art, science, literature, the onus of proof goes against it.
> ('The State', *SP*, p. 214)

Pound seems eclectic in his politics at this time, where communism and fascism were concerned. But, of course, both these tendencies had come out of socialism; it is only later that we begin to think of fascism as right and communism as left. He is disenchanted with France, Britain and his native country, giving vent to his dissatisfaction at this stage in his 1928 article 'Bureaucracy the Flail of Jehovah'. It appeared in the fourth and last issue of the journal *The Exile* that Pound had launched after coming to Rapallo. He had been complaining about bureaucrats in occasional letters to newspapers, especially about the introduction of passports, even while he was in London and continued when he moved to France, and in an article 'The Passport Nuisance' in *The Nation* in November 1927. In that article he complained about 'if not a new ruling class, at least a new bossiness' of passport officials. While still in London he had planned a trip to Paris with his wife. But there he met several objections from Passport Officers of the American Embassy. He 'was rescued by an elderly intelligent official from another department who took two hours off and swore to several contradictory statements in a manner showing great familiarity with the mind-ersatz of officialdom' (Stock, p. 224). But by now his dislike of bureaucrats takes on a bitter edge. The following excerpts are reproduced from the last few paragraphs of 'Bureaucracy the Flail of Jehovah':

> It is because the inspectors of the port of New York are told they represent justice that they behave like gorillas.
>
> The point of corollary here is that theoretical perfection in a government impels it ineluctably towards tyranny. In ancient days it was the divine descent of the ruler; in our time it is the theoretical justice or perfection of organism, the to, for and by the plebs, etc. that puts this more moral fervour and confidence in so dangerous a place, i.e., as powder in the cannon, and behind the projectile.
>
> Must we have bureaucrats? If we must have bureaucrats by all means let us treat them humanely; let us increase their

salaries, let us give them comforting pensions; let them be employed making concordances to Hiawatha, or in computing the number of sand-fleas to every mile of beach at Cape May, but under no circumstances allow them to do anything what bloody ever that brings them into contact with the citizen. The citizen should never meet or see an official in the exercise of its functions. Treat the bureaucrat with every consideration, and when he ultimately dies do not replace him.

The job of America for the next twenty years will be to drive back the government into its proper place, i.e., to force it to occupy itself solely with things which are the proper functions of government.

The qualifications of the ideal *fonctionnaire*, custom official or other are that he should be lazy, timid, have nice manners, no power, and a good deal of intelligence. The higher bureaucrats should be grounded in the TA HIO and in the analects of Confucius, apart from which they need only a specialist's 'education'. In the ideal state no Christian should ever be permitted to hold executive office. If the last proposition is not self-evident I am perfectly willing to debate it.

('Bureaucracy', *SP*, p. 220–1)

One way to read this is as a manifesto of a libertarian, but its idiosyncrasy, especially about Christians is a sign that the writer is beginning to leave the shores of rational discourse. Since Pound had not been back to America and had not encountered a New York port inspector for well over seventeen years by then, one wonders if he is reliving old grudges or inventing new ones or reporting what he has heard from friends. For a man about to be seduced by the leader of a fascist state, this is a puzzling piece. But it is yet another milestone on the way to the formulation of his dark vision.

Yet this dark vision cannot be attributed to any recent petty grievance. He had always been picking quarrels and starting campaigns. In 1926, he had become unhappy about copyright laws and in the wake of the controversy surrounding James Joyce's *Ulysses* on the grounds that it was pornographic, about pornography laws as well. But as Hemingway rightly said this was 'moonshine'; it did not trouble him much and he gave up the campaign just as he had many other such campaigns. He was enjoying recognition and success. The *Dial* magazine had given him an award for the year 1927 for his services to literature, which he insisted on interpreting as his *Cantos* or his poetry as a whole. This award of $2000 (about £55,000 in today's money) was most welcome as an investment for a future income of $100 per annum. His friend Wyndham Lewis wrote a tribute with the barbed title, 'The Revolutionary Simpleton'. But he did say of Pound that 'He has really walked with Sophocles beside the Aegean; he has *seen* the Florence of Cavalcanti; there is nowhere in the Past that he has not visited' (Stock, p. 271, quoting 'The Enemy', February 1927).

His attention turned to causes of war when the Carnegie Endowment for Peace published its *Report on the Effects of the War*. This is yet another milestone in the changing face of Ezra Pound. He wrote back to its Chairman saying that they should look at the causes rather than the effects of war. These were, he stated:

1. Manufacture and high pressure salesmanship of munitions, armaments etc.
2. Overproduction and dumping, leading to trade friction, etc. strife for markets etc.
3. The works of interested cliques, commercial, dynastic and bureaucratic. (*SP*, p. 222)

He went on to add in good muckraking fashion details of various deals which had been made by lobbies on behalf of armament manufacturers. He cites Sir Basil Zaharoff, the British arms merchant, as well as Vickers and Krupp for their activities in offloading arms on to *les nations jeunes*. He was to make Zaharoff a frequent butt of his caustic remarks as time went on, especially later, when Jews became for one reason or another his targets.

Yet, as the 1920s progressed, apart from his reviews of Douglas at the outset, he was not much concerned with economic matters. What we see in his correspondence and his writings is a man getting older and more cantankerous, pursuing some idiosyncratic schemes but nothing out of the ordinary given his past record. His biographer Noel Stock says of him at the end of his first five years in Rapallo, 'As his correspondence grew he began to think of himself more and more as a leader having a part to play in the affairs of his country' (Stock, p. 282).

He had been running the practical affairs of Eliot and Joyce and many other young contemporaries. Hemingway complained:

> So far, we have Pound the major poet devoting, say, one fifth of his time to poetry. With the rest of his time he tries to advance the fortunes, both material and artistic, of his friends. He defends them when they are attacked, he gets them into magazines and out of jail. He loans them money. He sells their pictures. He arranges concerts for them . . . He advances them hospital expenses and dissuades them from suicide . . .
> (Stock, p. 260)

From solving the mundane problems of his artist friends to solving America's was but a normal extension given the conceit of a forty-year-old genius. Yet it was soon to get out of hand.

The 1920s had started badly but a semblance of normality returned. Germany's currency had been repaired by an international loan and moderate prosperity had returned. America was enjoying the Roaring Twenties and while Prohibition made life difficult, speakeasies, flapper girls and jazz made it exciting as well. Britain had rejoined the Gold Standard in 1925 at a bad parity and this led to mass unemployment and the General Strike, but Pound seems to have taken little note of that. Mussolini had slowly consolidated his power but he was nowhere near to being the totalitarian dictator that he became in the 1930s.[7] The first five years that Pound spent in Rapallo, 1924 to 1929, were the best years of the inter-war period for Europe. Economic questions lay dormant in Europe as in Ezra Pound's mind.

It is the Great Depression which turns Ezra Pound into a full-time economic pamphleteer, and as he does this over the years, but especially after 1939, he becomes more bitter, more polemical and his vision gets darker. In 1933, he wrote a long pamphlet, *ABC of Economics*. This is the basic text which then gets embroidered and elaborated in various contexts over the next twelve years in 'Social Credit: An Impact' (1935), 'The Individual in his Milieu' (1935), which is about Silvio Gesell; 'What is Money For?' (1939); *A Visiting Card* (1942), *Gold and Work* (1944), 'America, Roosevelt and the Causes of the Present War' (1944), 'An Introduction to the Economic Nature of the United States' (1944). There were shorter items as well, which repeated the message of these longer pieces. After the Second World War and while Pound was in St Elizabeth's, six of these pamphlets were reissued by Peter Russell in London under the title *Money Pamphlets by £*. These were 'Social Credit: An Impact', 'What is Money for?', *Gold and Work*, *A Visiting Card*, 'The Economic Nature of the United States', 'America, Roosevelt and the Causes of the Present War'. His radio speeches made up a seventh item. These pamphlets constitute what Pound thought were his best prose works on money and economics.

There were also other writings, as well as the *Cantos*, of course. There was his writing on the theme of American culture – 'The Jefferson–Adams Letters as a Shrine and a Monument' (1937–8), and 'National Culture – A Manifesto' (1938). There were two obituary contributions on A. R. Orage and one on Ford Madox Ford, which touched on economic and cultural issues. Attacks on religion con-

---

7 See for a longer description of the economics and politics of 1924–9, my *Marx's Revenge*, pp. 152–7.

tinued in 'Terra Italica' (1931–2), 'Ecclesiastical History' (1934), 'Degrees of Honesty in Various Occidental Religions' (1939), 'Deus est Amor' (1940).

In this triangle of religion, culture and economics, themes overlap, allusions become more and more succinct and Latin, Greek, Old French and Italian expressions abound, footnote annotations are badly required. Pound is at once a lucid and a maddeningly obscure writer but since he is also repetitive you begin to get the hang of the recurring themes after a while. Douglas and the financial theoretician Silvio Gesell are cited frequently but there are other favourites whom one may never have heard of. Thus Marx often occurs in the company of Monsieur le Marquis de la Tour du Pin as two people who had the same blind spot about money. Arthur Kitson's evidence before the 1931 Macmillan Committee on Money and Industry is cited as final proof of the evils of banking, as is a letter by Henry Paterson, one of the founders of the Bank of England. There is a constant lament that Americans have neglected to publish with proper reverence the papers of past Presidents, especially Martin Van Buren. Yet these things are alluded to rather than explained.

But there is one unifying theme linking culture, religion and economy: usury. The decline of Christianity is traced to the repudiation of Canon Law. The reader has to infer that this refers to the prohibition on usury and this is why the Renaissance marks a watershed for Pound. Whatever was before, especially the Mediterranean civilization of the thirteenth and fourteenth centuries, was to be placed above the Renaissance and Christianity as it evolved after that. Calvin emerges as a villain. America's history is divided into the good days when Congress was in control of the money, and the days when bankers took over after the Civil War and the return of Gold and monetary orthodoxy. America was still in decline as far as Pound was concerned ever since the halcyon days of Jefferson and Adams, with Andrew Jackson being a sign of the last struggle against the bankers. This is not necessarily deep historical writing with footnotes and references. It is polemical writing, short and angry and obsessive. It is also in the tradition of American writings on the evil of banks as the enemy of the ordinary farmer and worker. A strand of American opinion has always held that banking is a species of fraud and the farther west and south you go from the eastern seaboard the more people hold it as an undisputable truth.

Thus from the start of the 1930s, Pound gets engaged in economic polemics and as time passes he gets more and more impatient and frustrated. There is, of course, a horrendous economic crisis in the West. Between the collapse of Wall Street in 1929 and America's entry into the Second World War in 1941, unemployment remained very high, not only in America but in many parts of Western Europe. Banks had failed in Austria and Germany, and unemployment rose all over the continent. Banks failed in the USA as well and Roosevelt's first act after taking office in 1933 was to declare a Banking Holiday; Congress began an inquiry into banks soon after. Britain was a slightly odd one out in this as it had experienced higher unemployment earlier than most due to the decision to restore the Gold Standard in 1925. But by the time the second Labour Government resigned in 1931 and was replaced by the National Government, things could begin to change for the better. The Gold Standard was abandoned and monetary discipline relaxed; a reduction in interest rates helped Britain to begin to recover in the early thirties. Yet this recovery was not as rapid as many would have wished. The general perception was of a deep crisis of capitalism.

The Soviet Union was seen to be enjoying planned economic growth with full employment. Germany, upon the advent of Hitler, abandoned free-market liberalism and adopted policies on the monetary and labour relations fronts which helped the economy to enjoy low levels of unemployment. Whatever the later atrocities of the Nazi rule, its economic record in the thirties was better than that of Britain or France. Italy had also adopted corporatist policies and by cutting wages and banning strikes, with tariffs and arms production, avoided the worst of the Depression. Faced with bank collapses, Mussolini set up financial institutions for the reconstruction of the economy – the Istituto per la Riconstruzione Italiano (IRI) and the Istituto Mobiliare Italiano. These gestures helped restore bank credits and revived industry and thus stabilized the Italian economy.[8]

Ezra Pound does not refer to these developments but he becomes more fond of Mussolini and even attributes to the Duce superior understanding of poetry after a meeting in January 1933 when Mussolini looked at a copy of *A Draft of XXX Cantos* and found it 'divertente' (Stock, p. 306). This was an example of reverse flattery wherein Pound saw more in Mussolini's gesture than was meant by the Duce. Yet he was not totally off-beam in admiring the decisiveness of Fascist policies. Later developments have devalued everything the Italian and German leaders did, even when some of it has been copied without attribution since. Corporatism became a very respectable economic philosophy counter to free-market liberalism among European socialists in the 1970s and 1980s, its undoubted Fascist origins being left unacknowledged. The financial institution set up by Mussolini – the IRI – had pride of place in post-war Italian economic revival. Planning in mixed economies was also pioneered by Nazi and Fascist economic policy-makers in a bid to challenge economic liberalism. It was enthusiastically copied in post-war years by the governments of developing countries as well as some European socialist parties.

Academic economics was also in turmoil at this time. In the

---

[8] Details of the economic developments of this period are in my *Marx's Revenge*, chapter 10, pp. 158–172. See also Kindleberger, Charles, *The World in Depression 1929 –1939*. See also Martin Clark, *Modern Italy*, second edition, 1995, pp. 263–7.

leading universities of the day – Harvard, Vienna, the LSE and much of Cambridge – liberal orthodoxy prevailed. Planning and corporatist interference with the free market were not approved of and unemployment was thought to be transitory while distortions were being phased out. Among academic economists, only Keynes in Cambridge was frantically searching for an alternative which would not only convince policy-makers but, more important, persuade his fellow economists that a totally different way of looking at the economy was possible and theoretically sound. There were, of course, quacks and 'miracle workers' who had the perfect solution to any and every economic complaint. There were also practical people who pretended that nothing very much had gone wrong which the smack of firm government could not put right. Economists were wont to ignore both these categories of people.

It never fails to astonish the practical people that economists set such a large store by their theories. The assumptions made are unrealistic, the argument often convoluted and, worse still, full of arcane algebra, the jargon impenetrable. Economists however are convinced and not without reason that if a cure for economic ills cannot be demonstrated to work in an unrealistic theoretical model, it is unlikely to work in practice. Conversely if some things seem to work in practice, there must be a sound theoretical argument behind its success or the success itself will be short-lived and more damaging than beneficial in the long run. The experience of the thirties is a living proof of that belief. There was no shortage of magic recipes for the solution of unemployment being touted at that time, Communists and socialists of various hues – syndicalists, guild socialists, Christian socialists as well as even more extreme free-marketers – were urging solutions. Major Douglas was a major player in this crowd, and he received plenty of criticism from communists and socialists, including Hugh Gaitskell, later Chancellor of the Exchequer and Leader of the Labour Party, who wrote a trenchant critique of him. But many of these responses were negative and polemical. Everyone argued why Douglas was wrong but still no one knew what the right answer was. It was only when Keynes came out with *The General Theory of Employment, Interest and Money* in 1936 that the theory was sorted out. It then took ten years and a war before his theories were implemented in practical policies and assured continued prosperity for the Western world for thirty years at a stretch.

Pound knew of Keynes but he does not seem to have followed the developments in academic arguments. Keynes remains someone he denounces frequently as part of the bankrupt science of economics. He sticks to Douglas and the critics of bankers that he has read throughout this period. He ignores the developments under New Deal since he loathes Roosevelt. The attack on bankers which took place in the USA in the early New Deal days passes him by. Programmes of work-generation – the Public Works Administration (PWA) and Work Progress (later Projects) Administration (WPA) – that the New Deal launched are also by and large absent in his polemics. The fact that Britain came off the Gold Standard in 1931 and that the USA began to control it after the International Economic Conference in 1934 and proceeded to fix the price of gold so as to devalue the dollar – policies similar to those he championed – are ignored or not appreciated. Indeed, Pound saw the dollar devaluation as a conspiracy by Rothschild to raise the price of gold. As far as he was concerned, the outlines of his critique fixed during the 1920s and pronounced in the 1930s and 1940s were unaffected by these developments. His mind was made up. He knew the problem and he had the solution.

So what was the problem and what was its solution?

III
The Trouble With Money

Money is at the centre of Pound's complaints – Money and Usury, or the charging of interest on debt. Pound is of course not unique in being troubled about these matters.

Money has troubled the human race ever since its advent and economists are also in constant ferment about its theoretical necessity and about the ways of managing money so as to ensure economic stability. Controversies about money are not just confined to economics but inhabit the realms of politics, the arts and literature as well as daily life. Money and its working are a mystery.

For all we know, the prevalence of money is as long as human history itself, in that money is like language, a social creation for convenience and communication. Of course language can be used to good as well as to evil purposes. Recall Caliban: 'You taught me language, and my profit on't/ Is, I know how to curse.' (*The Tempest*, I ii)

Money similarly has its useful and its pathological sides and which of the two sides prevails is not inherent to its nature qua money, but due to the wisdom or otherwise of human management of money. Yet there persists a strongly held belief that money is artificial, that it is a device which distorts human relations and indeed human nature; that there was once an age when there was no money but direct unmediated relationships between people based on 'real' worth and not on money values; that it is only by the abolition of money that we can re-establish that pristine era of a lost innocence or a futuristic utopia of Socialism.[1] Money puzzles the mind because its power seems to have no visible support. Why

---

1 For the anthropological research on the role of money in human societies, see Parry and Bloch, *Money and the Morality of Exchange* (1989).

should pieces of metal and, much worse, pieces of paper, command real resources way beyond their physical weight or apparent worth? What gives money value since it is pretty useless for anything other than buying things? Why does paper acquire value if it is printed with certain words but not others? Is gold more valuable if it is minted into coin rather than in lump form?

It is as a son of a mint assayor that Pound wrote:

> The genius can pay in nugget and in lump gold; it is not necessary that he bring up his knowledge into the mint of consciousness, stamp it into either the coin of conscientiously analysed form-detail knowledge or into the paper money of words before he transmit it.[2]

The distance between artistic endeavour and filthy lucre is thus unbridgeable. It is not that lump gold is better than gold coin or paper money that is at the centre of the argument. The genius produces lumps of gold – be they the *canzoni* of troubadours or the piece of marble sculpted into a cat by Gaudier-Brzeska. Exchanging his product for gold coin or paper notes does not value it into equivalents; it devalues it. It does that because once exchanged, the work is no longer unique; it has an equivalent expression. It has been translated into its other. It has been alienated from the genius and handed over to the mere consumer. The genius has been robbed but he cannot complain because it has all been done legally. Put it this way and Pound is close to the young Karl Marx of the *Economic and Philosophical Manuscripts* of 1844.

Artists, writers, musicians are notorious for their hostility to money and the moneyed. Once there was a time when royal, ecclesiastic or aristocratic patronage was essential to make art in any form possible. The painter and sculptor and the musician as well as the scribe enjoyed a safe living while they had the patron's plea-

2 Nicholls, pp. 27–8, quoting 'Art Notes' by 'B. H. Dias' (Ezra Pound) in *New Age* xxvi no.4, 27 November 1919.

sure. The patron was repaid in gratitude and often immortality by being sung or sculpted or painted. Sometime during the eighteenth century all this began to change. The writer as poet or as a harmless drudge began to have to fend for himself, out of pride or necessity. Samuel Johnson was able to denounce his patron, the Earl of Chesterfield, for his neglect but Oliver Goldsmith starved in a garret. Novels opened out a market that some could cater to but the readership of poetry remained select. Writers of the generation of Wordsworth and Coleridge had to rely on the reading public and could not hope for patronage of the old type. It was different for musicians such as Beethoven or Mozart or Handel who enjoyed lavish patronage from courts and courtiers. Even as late as the mid-nineteenth century, Turner had a patron. But after the 1850s, all arts became bereft of patrons; even painters – the Impressionists for instance – had to fall back on the market. It was to be nearly a hundred years before public, state or municipal, or corporate patronage of the arts became established.

Pound lived through this transitional period. The artist was alone, struggling to survive, eyeing the rich who would not host him and hating the commercial option of selling his wares to the masses. Art and Commerce had to cohabit, with Art being the weaker partner and rightly resentful. Being anti-commercial, anti-capitalist, anti-money became second nature to the artistic genius, a badge of honour. Yet the artist also knew that patronage for his talents was essential not only for his own survival but for the larger aim of sustaining a flourishing culture.

Roger Fry as an artist but with a scientist's training was one of the few who were able to analyse this transition for the arts from patronage to market. In his essay 'Art and Commerce',[3] Fry laments the modern bourgeois taste for the expensive but unadventurous

[3] Fry's essay was first published by Hogarth Press in 1926 but all his writings on art are conveniently collected in Goodwin, Craufurd D. (ed.) *Art and the Market: Roger Fry on Commerce in Art – Selected Writings.*

artefacts, which he calls 'opifacts'. 'An opifact, then, is any object made by man not for direct use but for gratification of those special feelings and desires, those various forms of ostentation . . .'

Art is rare and revolutionary, disturbing in many ways and not favoured by the market, which likes tame opifacts which are reproductions of the classics of the past.

> The opificer is, as a rule, a fairly good member of society. He conforms without much difficulty. The artist is an intolerant individualist claiming a kind of divine right to the convictions of his personal sensibility. Consequently we may say that some margin of personal liberty and some consciousness of personal worth are probably essential to this curious by-product of social life, and besides this there must be opportunity to work. (Goodwin, p. 112)

Fry locates this poverty of the genius artist to a lack of taste among the new rich. Once the Church and the King and the Lords are gone as patrons, we have the New Rich, the bourgeoisie who often lack confidence in their own taste. His observations are worth quoting in full.

> The nineteenth century in England and France was again a period of extraordinary commercial development and organization, but here we meet with a situation which is probably new in the history of art.
>
> The great wealth acquired by this civilization encouraged an enormous production of artefacts, but unlike the great commercials of the Renaissance, those of the nineteenth century showed a marked predilection for opifacts that did not even resemble works of art. In an earlier civilization this would have led to the total submergence of artists; we should have had a state of things like that which obtained generally in Egypt and Rome. But in the nineteenth century the sense of individual worth and independence had been highly developed in the

middle classes, and we have the curious phenomenon of the artist refusing to be suppressed, persisting in continuing his activities in spite of any discouragement, and in the face of the organized body of opificers. (Goodwin, pp. 115–16)

The emergence of the artist as 'an intolerant individualist' was not a separate phenomenon from the rise of commercialism. Modernity when it came to Europe came in a double movement towards the end of the eighteenth century. On the one hand was the rise of industrial capitalism, facilitating immense wealth accumulation. There was also the French Revolution with its Romantic appeal for the rebel and the awkward individual. It was as if Adam Smith and Jean-Jacques Rousseau had coordinated their assaults on the old order. Thenceforward, the artist as a Romantic rebel engaged in subverting Society (no doubt for its own good) but starving all the while became a fixture of bourgeois life. [4]

Roger Fry seems to capture the problem that troubled Ezra Pound better than he could himself. Pound does not seem to be aware of this essay by Roger Fry. In general, he, along with his friend Wyndham Lewis, was hostile to Fry and almost everyone else in Bloomsbury. Yet Pound's initial dissatisfaction with modern commercial civilization is precisely that artists do not get the support they deserve. He did not attribute this to a lack of taste though he did think that he alone could recognize truly great writing and spot the writers worth supporting. He sought a more general explanation of his complaint in the nature of money and the capitalist economy. This was to lead him into deep waters but that is not his fault, or at least he is not alone in so being led deep under some heavy swirls and eddies of theoretical confusion. It is the nature of money itself that is the problem.

Money facilitates exchange, as economists tell us. True, but could it be that exchange itself may not be the good thing it is

[4] See Jones, Howard Mumford, *Revolution and Romanticism* (1979).

claimed to be? In reducing things to a common equivalent, their identity and uniqueness are destroyed. This may not matter for mass-produced goods – cans of soup, say – which do not possess uniqueness in any case. Except that, even in this instance, a can of soup – Campbell's soup – may acquire a whole new rarity by being painted by Andy Warhol (however, Warhol himself expressed Pound's frustration with capitalism by mocking the uniqueness of his own genius and mass-producing his soup painting – an artist who would yet be an opificer).

Modern capitalism has made mass production possible and thereby raised standards of consumption across the entire developed world and a large part of the rest of the world too. So the market gains its power by reducing many things to a common reproducible state and then making them cheap and saleable for money. The compulsion to sell does not however stop with the common commodity. It extends itself to the bespoke and personalized goods as well. There are 'positional goods' which one alone can have such as an isolated beach but which lose charm when a stranger shares your possession. There is a price for such positional goods and indeed their price is part of their charm. But once priced any fool can have them as long as he has got the money. Even rare things need to be sold and selling makes them less rare. It is Iago who invites comparison between his good name and his purse when he remarks that if his purse is stolen it is nothing but if his good name is stolen he loses something that the thief does not gain by having.

As the commercial society advanced, names could also be bought and sold and reputations cashed in. The Augustan Age, which first felt the impact of the influx of treasure from the Iberian conquests of the Americas and Africa, began to feel the distorting effect of money on social mores and indeed the social structure itself.[5] This is when you begin to read complaints about the quick-

5 J. G. A. Pocock in his various books has studied this phenomenon. See among others, *Virtue, Commerce and History* (1976, 1985).

silver, almost feminine nature of monetary wealth which distorts the established hierarchy of status and subverts the accepted distinctions between good and bad taste.

Valuation can be by its very nature a destructive act even as it facilitates economic activity. I not only lose the uniqueness of my creation but I alienate it from myself – I give it away to the other who has destroyed its uniqueness by offering me a price. The dialectic of destruction of uniqueness and the creation of equivalence and the possibility of alienation lie at the heart of the exchange economy.

This was well expressed by Immanuel Kant in one of his early works: 'In the kingdom of wants everything has either *value* or *dignity*. Whatever has a value can be replaced by something else which is equivalent; whatever, on the other hand, is above all value and therefore admits of no equivalent has a dignity.'[6]

In many ways Pound was fighting for the dignity of his art and of every other artist's art. This was certainly at the heart of his initial despair about artists in America finding gainful employment. Later his concerns about money spilt over into broader issues and then into the contemporary politics of fascism. But the way he chose to fight and the allies he sought were no friendlier to his enterprise than to the fellow Americans against whom he was prepared to commit treason. He confused Italian corporatism for anti-capitalism. His confusions led to some beautiful poetry, much venomous prose and many interesting speculations about the nature of Money and the troubles it can cause.

But if Money is troubling, it still partakes of the solid material world. It is when it turns into Credit and breeds itself by attracting interest that Pound joins many in being baffled. Aristotle himself could not fathom why money, barren as it is, should bear fruit in

6 *Fundamental Principles of the Metaphysics of Morals*, 51, Thomas Abbott translation 1949, quoted by George Fletcher in *Our Secret Constitution*, p. 104.

the form of interest (*Politics*, I, x). It is the central mystery of centuries of speculation beginning with Ancient Greece and spanning the three great documents of Monotheism of the Middle East from the Old to the New Testament and onwards to the Koran (see the box below: 'Injunctions Against Usury'). Usury is a sin; it is an affront against God and the Natural Order. The message against usury and the abhorrent dislike of Money seem universal across time and space – a hint of a long-lost but immanent element of human nature.

Injunctions against Usury

Psalm 15:5
He that putteth not out his money to usury, nor taketh reward against the innocent. He that doeth these things shall never be moved.

Exodus 22:25
If thou lend money to any of my people that is poor by thee, thou shalt not be to him as a usurer, neither shalt thou lay upon him usury.

Leviticus 25:35–37
35 And if thy brother be waxen poor, and fallen in decay with thee; then thou shalt relieve him: yea, though he be a stranger, or a sojourner; that he may live with thee.
36 Take thou no usury of him, or increase: but fear thy God; that thy brother may live with thee.
37 Thou shalt not give him thy money upon usury, nor lend him thy victuals for increase.

Deutoronomy 15:7–10
7 If there be among you a poor man of one of thy brethren within any of thy gates in thy land which the Lord thy God giveth thee, thou shalt not harden thine heart, nor shut thine hand from thy poor brother:
8 But thou shalt open thine hand wide unto him, and shalt surely lend him sufficient for his need in that which he wanteth.
9 Beware that there be not a thought in thy wicked heart, saying, The seventh year, the year of release, is at hand; and thine eye be evil against thy poor brother, and thou givest him nought; and he cry unto the Lord against thee, and it be sin unto thee.
10 Thou shalt surely give him, and thine heart shall not be grieved when thou givest unto him: because that for this thing the Lord thy God shall bless thee in all thy works, and in all that thou puttest thine hand unto.

Ezekiel 18: 8–9
8 He that hath not given forth upon usury, neither hath taken any increase, that hath withdrawn his hand from iniquity, hath executed true judgment between man and man,
9 Hath walked in my statutes, and hath kept my judgments, to deal truly; he is just, he shall surely live saith the Lord God.

Luke 6: 35
But love ye your enemies, and do good, and lend, hoping for nothing again; and your reward shall be great, and ye shall be the children of the Highest: for he is kind unto the unthankful and to the evil.

The Koran (Penguin Classics edition, translation by N. J. Dawood)

The Cow 2: 275–278
Those that live on usury shall rise up before God like men whom Satan has demented by his touch; for they claim that trading is no different from usury. But God has permitted trading and made usury unlawful. He that has received an admonition from his Lord and mended his ways may keep his previous gains; God will be his judge. Those that turn back shall be the inmates of the Fire, wherein they shall abide for ever.

God has laid his curse on usury and blessed almsgiving with increase. God bears no love for the impious and the sinful. Those that have faith and do good works, attend to their prayers and render the alms levy, will be rewarded by their Lord and will have nothing to fear or to regret.

Believers have fear of God and waive what is still due to you from usury. If your faith be true; or war shall be declared against you by God and his Apostles. If you repent, you may retain your principal, suffering no loss and causing loss to none.

The Imrans 3: 131
Believers do not live on usury, doubling your wealth many times over. Have fear of God, that you may prosper. Guard yourselves against the Fire, prepared for the unbelievers.

Women 4: 159–162
Because of their iniquity, we forbade the Jews wholesome things, which were formerly allowed them; because time after time they have debarred others from the path of God; because they practise usury – although they were forbidden it – and cheat others of their possessions. Woeful punishment have we prepared for those that disbelieve. But those of them that have deep learning, and those that truly believe in what has been revealed to you and what was revealed before you; who attend to their prayers and render the alms levy and have faith in God and the Last Day – these shall be richly compensated.

But, of course, it is not so universal. This horror of usury and the unease about money stop somewhere west of the Red Sea. Neither Hinduism nor Buddhism, Jainism nor any of the Chinese or Japanese traditions share these attitudes. Nor, though this is a less well-explored subject, do any of the many religions of the western hemisphere in the pre-Columbine era. Why usury should be reviled in the Classical European philosophy and the Near Eastern religions but not in Eastern religions remains a puzzle. Many 'secular' explanations are possible. The Abrahamic religions were originally preached in small closely knit societies based on kinship where a stranger was very likely a distant cousin if not quite literally a brother. Good times and bad times could hit anyone; so behaving well while you are rich was an insurance against what might befall you when you were hit by misfortune. These were also societies where money as coins or precious metals must have been scarce and interest rates very high. Lending was hazardous and with scarce money, high interest rates were inevitable. If, on top of all this, there was little prospect of long-run growth in income or output of the whole society, where would anyone who had been compelled to borrow find the surplus to pay back the principal as well as interest?

Thus in these poor Middle Eastern desert societies, the borrower would most likely be someone in distress and not someone likely to invest the money in order to earn a profit. Consumption loans are the most difficult to pay back if incomes are stagnant, and hence it would be reasonable to insist on a zero interest rate for such loans. Later on as societies became more complex, there were possibilities of generating surplus through trade or investment – a possibility which seems alive in the context of the Koran, the Prophet himself being a merchant. Then usury becomes a more contested act and a share in any surplus (generated by investment of the money lent) becomes a consideration. These secular explanations were to figure later when medieval Europe began to handle trade and flows of precious metals on a large scale.

But as far as we are concerned, it is this Abrahamic injunction against the taking of interest which gives Ezra Pound's obsessions a deeper resonance, as for example in the famous Canto XLV – against *Usura*. If you speak merely of charging interest rates you have one effect. But speak of Usury, and you bring with you the thunder and lightning from the Bible and the Koran. To be fair, as we shall see later, Ezra Pound's concerns were of a more modern variety, and had to do with the way the state dealt with debt rather than the problems of borrowing by private individuals. He wanted the state not to borrow money at an interest since he surmised that this gave bankers their licence to make large fortunes. The economy thereby got into the grip of the bankers because of the interest-bearing nature of public debt. In this, his critique of usury parts company with the religious injunction, but he himself did not highlight the difference sufficiently (nor indeed was aware of it) to avoid the charge that while he detested Christianity and Judaism, he shared their anti-usury sentiments.

This confusion of Pound's modern attack on bankers and governments with the age-old injunctions against usury led him, as we shall see later in more detail, into his anti-Semitism. The Christian injunction against usury derived from the Sermon on the Mount is much more severe and unconditional against taking interest than the Old Testament doctrine, which is against charging interest to your brothers but not to the people who are outside Judaism. The Christian doctrine is about justice and regards any charging of interest, any gain from lending as sinful, though it has to be said that St Thomas Aquinas took the view that this was a counsel of Christ not binding on everyone, supererogatory and not essential for salvation. But his was a later interpretation. The doctrine of usury was firmly established in St Augustine's works, and used as a weapon against the Jews in medieval Europe. Usury is a sin as far as the Catholic Church of the first millennium after Christ was concerned.

Aristotle's work was not known to the Christian Fathers of the first millennium but he also seems to come out against usury though for different reasons. He approves of money as a medium of exchange since in his view trade maintains the self-sufficiency of human societies. So money is good when it merely serves as a medium of exchange. He also approves of the accumulation of goods – Chrematistics – as long as such increase is a result of forces of Nature: 'We conclude therefore that the form of acquisition of goods that depends on crop and animal husbandry is for all men in accordance with nature.'

The problem comes from acquisition facilitated by use of money to make more money. This is contrary to Nature since money cannot breed money.

> ... The other (form of acquisition) which is to do with trade and depends on exchange is justly regarded with disapproval since it arises not from nature but from men's gaining from each other. Very much disliked also is the practice of charging interest; and the dislike is fully justified, for the gain arises out of currency itself, not as a product of that which currency was provided. Currency was intended to be a means of exchange, whereas interest represents an increase in the currency itself. Hence its name [*tokos*, meaning 'offspring' in Greek] for each animal produces its like, and interest is currency born of currency. And so of all types of business this is the most contrary to nature. (Aristotle, *Politics*, I, x; Penguin Classics edition, p. 87)

Neither the religious injunction nor Aristotle's philosophical objection against usury was, however, quite practicable. Outside simple primitive societies that are totally self-sufficient as well as closed, money has its uses. In a world of even moderate uncertainty, people want to provide against the proverbial 'rainy day'. Money is more than a medium of exchange. Money proves to be a good 'store of value', i.e. it is likely to be as useful today as tomorrow, though that is not to imply that it will have the same purchasing power always. So people put money by to spend on a future occasion. But one problem with money is that it is anonymous – my name is not on the gold coins I carry. Anyone can steal my money and it would be difficult to prove that it was mine. Hence money needs careful tending.

This is why rather than laying it by as an idle hoard (which could be stolen), people begin to entrust it to a goldsmith who can look after it. The goldsmith in turn can lend it to whoever has an immediate need of the money for business purposes. Later still the goldsmith lends not gold but a piece of paper which authorizes the borrower to 'draw' upon his loan. Thus are born banking and cheques. Soon we see a big pyramid of credit built on a slim foundation of gold or any other form of currency. The borrower spends his loan to start a business or expand it and his payments circulate around the economy lubricating commerce; or perhaps he uses the money to buy livestock or seeds to sow. In such cases increase and proliferation are implied – commerce leads to further commerce, livestock breed and plants yield crops. So if money earns an interest it is by being engaged in – or being advanced for – activities which in themselves create surplus. As Marx would put it, money bears interest when it takes the form of capital and it is money as capital which by employing labour creates the surplus which affords the interest.

Then again there are other uses of money. Within your village, you are well known and people will be willing to give you things or take things from you because they know you and trust you. They know your pedigree, your occupation, your worth. If you leave your village community, however, and encounter strange people who do not know you, you can transact with them only if you have something to give in exchange that they find desirable. If I have money they need not know me, my caste or my pedigree – my money is my bond.[7] Money is a substitute for trust as much as it is an insurance against the stranger or an uncertain future. Both the future and the stranger are unknown and money acts as a hedge against the unknown, a compensation for our ignorance.

And humankind found out that barter has its limits, and, as the economy spreads either in territory or in the range of products for sale and purchase, money comes in useful. The stranger may not want my wares though I may want his. He wants something from another stranger who has what he wants but can't get it because that stranger does not want his goods, and so on. If I offer money which is a 'universal equivalent' then my task is accomplished. If I do not have money I may be able to offer a 'promissory note'. Again, if the stranger trusts me, fine; if not he may ask for a premium above today's price to compensate for the risk that I may abscond. In complex societies money or even the promise of money can be vital. But then, what of God's injunction against usury?

Thus it was that medieval theologians and scholars found themselves struggling with the everyday inquiries of their flock about the injunction against usury. The widow who could not work herself but had some money to lend, perhaps to a banker in return for interest – how was she to live if she could not earn the return? What about mortgages?

St Thomas Aquinas first liberalized the doctrine of usury. St Augustine had declared that property was a human rather than a natural creation and hence partook of the degraded condition of all things human after the Fall. William of Auxerre first argued that it was precisely because of the Fall that Nature permitted private

---

[7] In the middle of writing this book I made a bid for a house in North London. The vendor wanted me to seal my bid with £1000 in *cash* because they had no guarantee that I would not renege, not having seen me in person.

ownership and St Thomas added that rational reflection in the Fallen state showed the necessity of private property.[8]

It was in Italy during the twelfth and thirteenth centuries that the first modern developments in trade and banking took place. For a thousand years before that Europe had been drained of gold and silver as it ran a deficit in trade with Asia. The sheer scarcity of coin and the breakdown of Roman rule made for extremely high interest rates and gave power to the Church to intervene in money matters. This situation was altered as treasure began to come to Europe first as trade surplus and then from the Iberian conquest of colonies in Africa and the Americas, and Venice and other Italian towns began a lucrative trade, which in time led to money lending.

The issue that successive generations of scholastic writers had to tackle was of the legitimacy of money made by 'advancing' money. Jews were not prohibited by the Christian doctrine of usury and from earliest times the money-lending Jew figured prominently in Christian anti-Semitism. In the early centuries of the second millennium, Lombards in Northern Italy began to trade in the coin of Venice and other Italian city states. This allowed them to disguise the trade as being not in money but in foreign exchange. Lombards were thus the pioneer bankers among Christians. But in the main it was the Jew who bore the opprobrium of being the dealer in money. In Elizabethan times in England this was most famously characterized in *The Merchant of Venice*.[9] But by then the Church had begun to understand that profit and interest were two related but separate categories. Money was not always barren; it could fructify by being put to use. The borrower was not always a helpless impoverished person whom the lender could milk. He could be an enterprising mer-

8 This can only be a brief discussion of the vast subject of the doctrine on usury. See John T. Noonan, *The Scholastic Analysis of Usury*, 1957.
9 There is more to *The Merchant* than merely anti-Semitism. See for an incisive analysis of the role of money in the play, Buchan, James, *Frozen Desire*, 1997, pp. 87–92.

chant who would stock a ship sailing away to the Orient and make money by selling and buying. This is the case of Antonio in *The Merchant of Venice*. Antonio stands guarantee for his friend Bassanio who needs money to court Portia and gets it from Shylock but at a bizarre price. This is a consumption loan at one level but since Portia is rich, who is to say that Bassanio is not making an investment in his own future prosperity as well as happiness? There were rewards of risk taking and costs – legitimate charges for insurance. Not all these payments were on a par with usury. The injunction in Islam against *riba* is similar and a share of profits is allowed as legitimate, but not a fixed charging of interest on debt.[10]

Keynes in the concluding chapters of his *General Theory of Employment Interest and Money* speculated about the doctrine of usury and in his own iconoclastic way saw some merit in it. He could see the justification for the ban in the conditions of the economy of those times.

> The destruction of the inducement to invest by an excessive liquidity-preference was the outstanding evil, the prime impediment to the growth of wealth, in the ancient and medieval worlds. And naturally so, since certain of the risks and hazards of economic life diminish the marginal efficiency of capital whilst others serve to increase the preference for liquidity. In a world, therefore, which no one reckoned to be safe, it was almost inevitable that the rate of interest, unless it was curbed by every instrument at the disposal of society, would

10 St Thomas Aquinas recognizes the return to risk when he states that 'he who entrusts his money to a merchant or craftsman so as to form a kind of company does not transfer the ownership of his money to him. Rather, it remains his, so that it is at his risk that the merchant speculates with it, or the craftsman uses it for his work; and so the lender may lawfully demand, as something belonging to him, a share of the profits derived from the money' (*Summa Theologica* 5(b), art. 2 /ad. 5; IIaIIae 78; Cambridge Texts, 2002, 228–9). The issue of the usury ban in Islam is another very big one and I do not deal with it here, but see the recent story about 'Sharia compliant financing' in the *Financial Times* 13 August 2003.

> rise too high to permit of an adequate inducement to invest.
>
> ... I was brought up to believe that the attitude of the Medieval Church to the rate of interest was inherently absurd, and that the subtle discussions aimed at distinguishing the return on money-loans from the return to active investment were merely Jesuitical attempts to find a practical escape from a foolish theory. But I now read these discussions as an honest intellectual effort to keep separate what the classical theory has inextricably confused together, namely, the rate of interest and the marginal efficiency of capital. For it now seems clear that the disquisitions of the schoolmen were directed towards the elucidations of a formula which should allow the schedule of the marginal efficiency of capital to be high, whilst using rule and custom and the moral law to keep down the rate of interest. (*GT*, pp. 351–2)

Modern capitalism's origin was in merchant capital and then it developed into industrial and now knowledge capital. Throughout its history, it has been helped by the ability of the risk-taking, enterprising person – the entrepreneur – to borrow money at interest and convert it into profit by *investment*. It was when economists following Adam Smith began to analyse the nature of modern capitalism that the distinction between profits and interest was properly understood. The usury ban was then criticized by economists as they could show that money borrowed could bear fruit as profit which in turn was a reward for risk taking and enterprise.

Even then the role of money was not fully understood and economists preferred to analyse the economy in 'real' i.e. moneyless terms. Thus in David Ricardo's economics, money plays an epiphenomenal role. The real economy can exist without money, being driven by real wages and real profits, while the amount of money merely determines the level of absolute prices. Karl Marx was the first of the political economists who understood the nature of money in a capitalist system. When he started his study of political economy in the 1840s, his first reactions to money were similar to Ezra Pound's since he came to economics from philosophy. It was after a lifetime of study and thinking that he understood the nature of modern capitalism and the centrality of profits. He appreciated the role of money in capitalism best of all economists when he said that money takes the form of capital when it is advanced by the capitalist-producer. If money is not so advanced but used for personal consumption then it is merely money as purchasing power and creates no surplus even if while spending the money I employ someone. That person performs unproductive labour though he or she may satisfy my wants. But the person engaged by the capitalist performs productive labour since he or she creates surplus during production-surplus that takes the form of surplus value and then money profit in turn.[11]

Thus theologians were early pioneers in separating the concept of profit from that of interest, and saw that the legitimacy of interest payments derived from the use of money lent in generating profit by productive investment. Thus the notion of usury as such can only be applied to consumption loans which generate no surplus while making use of the money borrowed. But even that is simplistic when it comes to buying durable goods by means of a loan. Modern economics takes the view that borrowing for consumption — as in, for example, taking out a mortgage to buy a house for dwelling in — is merely a rearrangement of income flows and consumption flows. When I take a mortgage I am borrowing against my future income flows to bring my consumption of housing nearer the present. But then I am doing more than consuming. I am building up my portfolio of assets by acquiring a house on mortgage. So the onus of public disapproval for interest charging falls residually on loans given for current nondurable consumption to the very poor and hard-up who are not borrowing against a

11 I have explained this in *Marxian Economics* and in *Marx's Revenge*.

rising income in the future but desperately living from hand to mouth. And indeed it is precisely in this sector of the poor assetless consumer that the loan sharks thrive.

Of course, the matter is not so straightforward since even among economists there are differences, and economics does not command universal respect. One may admit the legitimacy of charging interest and still complain about the height of the rate of interest charged. Banks come in for frequent criticism for paying paltry amounts of interest, if any, to their depositors for money kept in the bank vaults, and turn around to charge high rates if the same depositors borrow money by going into the red. Mortgage payments amount to a multiple of the sum originally borrowed and this in itself perplexes people. In the popular imagination this is robbery even though it is implicit in the nature of long-term borrowing. Many non-governmental organizations protest about borrowing by poor countries from the international financial institutions – the World Bank or the IMF – or foreign governments, which leaves these poor countries with a large burden of debt. The *moral case* for charging interest especially to the poor, be they people or nations, is still not proven.[12] This is even more so if the original borrowing has been frittered away by the person/nation and the repayment falls on a subsequent heir or government. The burden of debt repayment may make survival difficult even at the lowest levels of living. This is again because we are happy if interest is paid out of 'surplus' but not if it comes out of necessary consumption.

Economists and bankers and 'policy makers' answer these objections by retorting that if every loan that proved burdensome was cancelled then borrowers would have no incentive to behave responsibly. This would be a case of moral hazard where the contract is so framed as to give incentives to one of the parties to the

12 See a recent attack on the debt problem in Hertz, *IOU: The Debt Threat and Why We Must Defuse It* (2004).

contract for non-compliance. As a consequence the future flow of lending may also dry up. So in the discussions during the late 1990s and early 2000s about relieving the burden of debt on poor countries, conditions were made that, if debt forgiveness is granted, the money thus saved would be used for the poorest residing within these poor countries and not spent on luxuries for the elite or for arms purchases. Such conditionality is attacked as an assault on the sovereignty of the borrowing countries – but ultimately the old adage 'Beggars can't be choosers' applies. In practice contracts are renegotiated, debts restructured or written off and in fact interest charges are reduced *ex-post facto*. Indeed the debt that countries owed to private commercial banks in the wake of petrodollar recycling in the 1970s and 1980s was written off as bad debt or repaid as a fraction of the original sum.

Usury thus remains a live issue perhaps not arousing quite the moral fervour that it once evoked and certainly not with the virulence that Ezra Pound brought to it. And yet it has a long and respectable pedigree as far as real-world rather than economic theory is concerned. Within economics, there is no agreed theory of interest. In mainstream economics interest has little to do with money. In classical and neo-classical theories, there is no role for money in the economy except as an epiphenomenal determinant of the absolute level of nominal prices. As far as economic theory is concerned, the interest rate is a price of real savings and real investment, with the forces of productivity determining the demand for capital as investment and the habit of thrift supplying the savings to match the investment. This analytical structure gives no role to money or banks. Keynes proposed a purely monetary theory of interest in which it was the liquidity of money, the ability of ready cash to be immediately used for purchases, that commands a price which holders of money demand if they are to part with it. This is a purely short-run theory for interest rates while the classical and neoclassical theories are for the long run.

Thus a single theory of interest rate which will cover the short and the long run remains elusive.

A heroic effort to provide a modern theory of interest was made in the 1950s by the American Nobel Prize-winning economist Paul Anthony Samuelson, whose argument was based on the obligations each generation owes to its parent generation to take care of it.[13] So my savings while I am working feed my parents since their savings fed their parents. It is very much an Old Testament-type argument about lending within the family. At the end of the day in such an intergenerational arrangement no savings need be actually made as long as I take care of my parents and no interest need be paid either. And of course money is not involved in the argument. So we remain with Keynes's view of interest as a monetary phenomenon and the neoclassical view of interest as 'real' i.e. non-monetary. What there is perhaps some agreement on is a theory of the term structure of interest rates, i.e. why short-run rates differ from long-run rates.[14]

The height of interest rates at any time is influenced by supply and demand – the supply of credit, which is determined by the banks and the policy of monetary authorities, and the demand for credit which comes from businesses in the various activities. Yet the suppliers – the banks – are few and the borrowers many. The supplier has the advantage of controlling what the borrower wants. There is a persistent opinion among the borrowers that suppliers abuse their power which derives from the fewness of their numbers and the concentration of credit in their hands –

---

13 Samuelson, Paul, 'An Exact Consumption Loan Model of Interest Without the Social Contrivance of Money', *Journal of Political Economy*, December 1958, pp. 467–82.

14 *The New Palgrave Dictionary of Economics* published in 1987 has an entry on 'Interest Rates' by J. E. Ingersoll, which is all about the term structure but does not discuss why there is a positive interest rate at all. A neighbouring entry on 'Interest and Profit' by Carlo Panico is closer to the view taken here.

their 'oligopoly' power. Thus despite competition between the credit givers, eventually the creditor has the upper hand. This is why banks and financial markets need regulation. Nowadays banks are regulated either by a Central Bank or a Financial Regulator but this has been a slow realization after decades of powerful lobbying against regulation by the bankers despite popular feeling that somehow banks should be brought under popular control. This was definitely the sentiment in America in the late nineteenth century when the movement against the resumption of Gold payment was popular in the West and the South among farmers and small businessmen. This was the root of William Jennings Bryan's Cross of Gold speech. Thirty years after that Winston Churchill, while Chancellor of the Exchequer, wished that he could make the Bank of England see some sense on charging lower interest rates. In a memo to his chief civil servant he noted, 'The Governor [of the Bank of England] allows himself to be perfectly happy in the spectacle of Britain possessing the finest credit in the world simultaneously with a million and a quarter unemployed . . . I would rather see Finance less proud and Industry more content' (Skidelsky II, 1992, p. 198).

In English political discourse there is a long-standing, if somewhat maverick, tradition of being anti-banking and anti-debt.[15] There is a story which reads like a conspiracy theory as to how Charles II was deprived of money by a Parliament that would not let him tax; and neither could he borrow money from the City. But after the Bloodless Revolution of 1688 which removed the Stuart kings, the prince who was invited to take up the throne – William of Orange – faced the same problem. The conspiracy theory then alleges that the Bank of England was granted its Charter in 1694 to

---

[15] This discussion is based on Hollis, Christopher, *The Two Nations: A Financial Study of English History* (1935; reissued 2005). It is not that this is the most accurate account but it is one that Ezra Pound read and was much influenced by.

render the Crown free of its dependence on Parliament, but it would do this by vesting power in the hands of a small number of rich City merchants who were shareholders of the Bank. This is because the Bank would lend money up to £1.2 million to the Crown in return for the privilege of issuing its own notes. These notes would be redeemable in gold, but, as long as they circulated, they saved gold from being in circulation. The longer-run effect of the Bank, in fact, was to bring interest rates down in England relative to France, and usher in a Financial Revolution, a factor which was to be crucial in the ascendancy of England over France during the long century between 1688 and 1815.

For the conspiratorially minded, however, the Bank was the beginning of the rule by the City of London and a licence to make lots of money. Ezra Pound repeatedly cites a letter of William Paterson, who was a sort of venture capitalist of his days. His prospectus for the Bank eventually formed the basis of the Parliamentary legislation establishing the Bank. Pound frequently quotes Paterson as saying, 'The bank has the benefit of interest on all moneys it has created out of nothing.'[16] This for Pound means that banks create profits out of nothing. This is a common fallacy about how banks operate. Banks have to be prudent to be able to command the confidence of depositors and thus have collateral assets against any credit they create by lending. In the feverish imagination of anti-banking agitators, banks make large profits. But a look at the prof-

16 Pound, *A Visiting Card* (1952; published as *Carta da Visita* in 1942), pamphlet, p. 9; I have tried to trace this quote but despite trying every source for Paterson have not been able to do so. Pound quotes Hollis but Hollis does not give the source for his quote. It is not in the *Proposal: A Brief Account of the intended Bank of England*, published in 1694, whose author is cited as Paterson or Michael Godfrey. I have also checked a biography of Paterson with no success. But this claim is not implausible for a prospectus writer to insert in an original bid to attract support. Paterson resigned from the Board of Directors of the Bank soon after its founding and went on to launch the Darien scheme (a plan to establish a commercial settlement in Panama), a venture that, unlike the Bank, failed.

it record of the Bank of England will show that the Bank made modest profits. Its dividends are a matter of public record and amount to around 4 to 5 per cent in the first twenty years after establishment and decline to 3 to 4 per cent in much of the eighteenth century.[17] Profits in banking are seldom excessive and shares in banks rarely perform spectacularly as any inspection of financial history will show. This is not to say that popular imagination will ever be convinced that banking is legitimate business.

The conspiracy of the City against the Country was, according to the anti-Bank forces, compounded when Walpole as Prime Minister established the National Debt with a sinking fund to service the debt charges. The ability of the government to borrow money at will was seen by the losers in the 1688 Settlement – the Jacobites and the Tories – as the fountain of corruption and growth of arbitrary power. But of course the debt had to be serviced, and Parliament had to vote the taxes to service the debt. The Prime Minister had powers of patronage, and it was alleged, through the National Debt, filthy lucre to bribe Parliamentarians to vote for the taxes. Thus evolved the critique of Old Corruption which William Cobbett took up in the nineteenth century. Such criticism had particular force then because the inflationary years of the Napoleonic Wars were turned into deflation by the Bank of England restoring the pound at its original Gold parity. Deflation always makes borrowers unhappy just as creditors fear inflation.

Eventually, of course, Parliament brought the Bank of England under another bout of supervision. The Banking Act of 1844 was hotly debated and pamphlets poured out from rival theorists as to the best way of regulating the Bank. The Bank had a monopoly of note issue in England. It also created credit by discounting bills of exchange – promissory notes – which traders presented before it.

17 Dividends of the Bank of England for the first hundred years are given in Clapham, *The Bank of England: A History* Vol. 1 (1944), Appendix B, p. 292.

Of course, the Bank could discount unlimited pieces of such paper since it could meet any claims for cash payment by issuing its own notes. One side wanted to control the power of the Bank to issue excess credit, since it could cause inflation and lead to cycles of boom and bust. This required a check on how the monopoly of currency issue was used, and keeping the currency-issuing division of the Bank separate from its banking, i.e., credit-creating, division. Currency could henceforth only be issued against gold reserves. Credit had to be backed by collateral of 'sound' paper – i.e., bills of exchange issued for genuine trading purposes. By separating the two divisions, the Bank would be forced to discount only such paper which it could honour without printing its own notes.

But merchants wanted more, not less, credit, and cheaper credit too. They refuted any notion of excess credit. Whatever paper the Bank discounted – lent against – was obviously for legitimate needs of trade. Why else would it be issued? Merchants and traders, being borrowers, liked inflation which reduced the real burden of repayment. They complained that restricting credit harmed trade, created unemployment and drove businesses into bankruptcy. Orthodox financial groups, on the other hand, wanted their assets safe against inflation and they favoured strict regulation. They won. Yet the controversy between the Banking School and the Currency School, as the orthodox and the expansionist sides became known, recurs in economics to this day.

The English anti-banking tradition is not nearly as populist as its American variant. Pound was to be beguiled by it, but then his American background had prepared him for it. In any case the nationalization of the Bank of England in 1945 took much of the sting out of the suspicion that the Bank was a cabal of private financiers holding the government of the day to ransom. Yet financial orthodoxy continued to have its sway and credit restrictions were as frequent as ever, even after the nationalization of the Bank.

There is still a tradition of City versus Industry, and private commercial banks still excite some political opposition. But the Old Labour demands for 'taking over the City as soon as possible' have receded. What we have instead nowadays are anti-globalization marchers attacking the buildings in the City as a gesture of protest. The economic rationale for banks remains for many a mystery, while the weakness of the moral case for charging interest rates especially to the poorest today provides a focal point for the Global Justice movement under its anti-usury banner.

The American story of money and banks and their evil influence is a much richer affair. In colonial times, individual colonies often issued their own money since the inflow of gold coins from England was uncertain and the needs of trade had to be met. The Board of Trade in London regulated the powers of colonies to issue currency by getting Parliament to pass orders against such practices. But a disregard for orthodox finance characterized those early days. When the War of Independence broke out in 1775, the rebels, to provision their army, had to issue paper backed solely by a promise to redeem it in the future, after victory had been won. While the war lasted, much paper was issued and as happens in wartime, there was rampant inflation. Farmers got into debts which were not easy to repay. When war ended and prices fell, there was much unrest, of which Shays' Rebellion was the most famous manifestation, alarming many people by its attack on the notion of private property itself. The new Republic was established to protect private property, not denounce it, and whatever the popular sentiments of indebted farmers, taxes had to be paid and debts honoured.

Alexander Hamilton as the first Secretary of the Treasury of the Republic resolved to honour all the paper issued by the Revolutionary Army as well as all the paper issued by the individual states. By this time, the early 1790s, much of that paper was circulating at a fraction of its nominal value as no one thought it would ever be redeemed. Those who held the paper, and many Congressmen were among them, had a bonanza when Hamilton undertook to repay all such paper at par value. This was resented by his colleagues especially Jefferson and Madison who smelt financial orthodoxy of the British variety. But Hamilton wanted to establish the creditworthiness of the new Republic both within the country and abroad. In this, he was successful. He also helped create the first Bank of the United States, a national bank which could be a creditor for the government. Renewal of the Bank's Charter by the Congress became a recurring battle where the Jeffersonians pitted themselves against the Federalists, who had orthodox beliefs about finance. On one hand was the orthodox idea that a National Debt should be created which would be serviced by the tax revenue. Such was the English arrangement and this made credit cheap for the government. Against this was Jefferson's idea that no permanent debt should be created, and if the government had to borrow, the paper should be bought back by paying out of tax revenue. No interest would be paid on government paper while it was held by any citizen. Of course his radical ideas about finance did not prevent Jefferson from taking a loan from the Rothschilds when he purchased Louisiana from the French.

A celebrated battle between Bank and Executive took place when Andrew Jackson became President in 1828. His election was the first time the old elite failed to elect one of their own to the Presidency. John Quincy Adams, the son of John Adams, second President of the Republic, lost after just one term. Jackson's election brought the newly settled areas of the West (what is now the Midwest) into prominence. Nicholas Biddle as the man behind the Bank became the classic antagonist of Jackson. Jackson defeated Biddle's attempts to obtain a new charter for his Bank. The Bank received the government's gold deposits as the sole banker and issued its own notes which were legal tender. It also acted as a central bank regulating the affairs of the many State banks which had been chartered and could issue their own notes (which, however, had to be redeemable in gold).

There was much resentment that the Bank, a privately owned monopoly, would challenge the elected power. Many on the Frontier liked cheap credit but Jackson himself was a hard money man. He wanted to have only gold and silver circulating as currency and not Bank of America notes. So he vetoed the renewal of the Charter and took deposits away from Biddle's Bank and gave them to State banks. While this deprived Biddle of his gold deposits, it also removed any control over the State banks in their credit creation. This led to a credit boom which in its turn collapsed after a couple of years. Martin Van Buren, who succeeded Jackson, took the control of currency back into the hands of the Federal Government by keeping the government's gold within its own control and minting coinage as and when required. No bank notes were henceforth legal tender. In a way Van Buren did what all modern governments do: control currency themselves rather than through the note issue of banks.

During the Civil War, the Federal Government issued its own paper currency without any gold backing. These 'greenbacks' were paper dollars issued much as was the paper during the Revolutionary War to provision the fighting forces. Again there was inflation and yet again farmers borrowed much money to expand their operations. When the war ended, there were immediate demands that the greenbacks be redeemed in gold. But gold was short and silver plenty. Those who feared a deflation preferred silver currency. But the American economy was growing rapidly and needed foreign capital to fuel the growth. Those who wished to borrow abroad preferred gold. After a prolonged battle lasting a decade, the gold interests won and Resumption became the law in 1877. Yet again the battle was between the orthodox finance interests, who wanted sound money and low inflation, and those who wanted cheap credit and did not mind if inflation broke out. It was Gold versus Silver, East Coast against the Rest. William Jennings Bryan was the hero of the unorthodox and he fought for the Presidency thrice on a reflationist ticket and lost all three times. Frank Baum's classic *The Wizard of Oz* is a parable of this episode with the Wizard being Bryan, as one who raised many false hopes but was ultimately found to be a weak man.

At the time, America did not have a central bank on the lines of the Bank of England. There were stock-market panics and crashes, leading to a shortage of liquidity and a run on the banks. During such a crisis in Britain, when a London bank was about to fail, the Bank of England was there to take on the role as 'lender of the last resort', which would save the bank and end the crisis. Since America, however, did not have such a central bank, there was much distress. After a severe crisis in 1909, the Federal Reserve System was set up in 1911 and soon became indispensable in providing sound credit to American businesses. But sound money was always equated with the East Coast plutocracy in American popular imagination, and banks remained under suspicion. Americans at the grass roots preferred their silver dollars.

Yet another deflationary crisis took place during the Great Depression. Many farmers faced foreclosure on their mortgages and were dispossessed. Banks were also failing in large numbers. Roosevelt declared a four-day 'banking holiday' immediately upon assuming Presidency in 1933 and set about a sweeping programme of reforms. Congressional hearings were called, and legislation passed, restricting the powers of banks to pursue financial activities other than deposit-taking and loan-issuing. Compared to British banks, American banks were severely regulated and no branch banking was possible at a national level.

After the Second World War, the Federal Reserve was also brought under stricter control of the Congress. Only during the 1970s were restrictions on American banks removed. But then during the 1980s, reminiscent of the old days, America had the massive failure of the Savings and Loan Associations, which left a number of small depositors poorer. Thus it continues. In American popular imagination, banks and bankers remain villains.[18]

Thus money and credit remain contentious topics. Economists pretend in each generation that there is nothing mysterious about money if only people will think rationally. Yet among them periodically fierce controversies break out. One generation's truths become the fallacies of the next one. Even during the last twenty-five years we have swung from regarding inflation as the greatest danger and calling for the governments to control their budget deficits and thereby make it easier for the central banks to control money supply, to the current fear of deflation and the policy rule that the central banks should control interest rates rather than money supply. In the twenty-five years before that, money was thought to be unimportant and the fiscal policy of the government – taxes and expenditure – everything. Budget deficits were disregarded and National Debt relegated to esoterica. At each stage people have mouthed conventional wisdom with no acknowledgement that it is the opposite of what was said before. Many a monetary theorist can be found lamenting that the subject of money lacks any foundations.

At the same time, central bankers are enjoying an immense power over economies since everywhere they are being given independence from politicians. Issues which should be trivial for an economics textbook such as changing over from one currency to another at a fixed rate – e.g. changing from French francs to Euros – excite controversies and popular disaffection for years after the change. Economists would say that the change is no more significant than changing from Fahrenheit to Celsius in weather reports, and yet the popular reaction to these changes is never quiescent. Money cranks, especially, have a great deal to say – but

[18] John Kenneth Galbraith reflects this suspicion of bankers in his writings. See his *Money: Whence It Came, Where It Went* (1975).

being a crank is no bad thing when it concerns a powerful force such as money. Ezra Pound was neither the first nor the last of the species, and in the next chapter I examine Pound's crankiness about money.

IV
Pound on Pound

After the Second World War Ezra Pound's pamphlets on money were, as I mentioned above, reissued by Peter Russell under the series title *Money Pamphlets by £*, six of them concerning monetary topics, broadly speaking, and a seventh pamphlet consisting of a selection of his radio speeches. His first large piece of economic writing, *ABC of Economics* (1933), a collection of essays, was not issued again but is available in his *Selected Prose*. There are of course other writings pursuing themes in which Pound dabbled, but it is to economics that he always returns. In his essays and articles, there are themes, and indeed sentences, that recur. He cannot let go of certain themes, and does not update or change his views in light of whatever might have happened. Thus his views on the New Deal continue to be hostile even when it is clear to his fellow monetary heretics, such as Christopher Hollis, that Roosevelt is against the banks and for sound economic policies.

Of course, Pound's primary concern from 1911 onwards was the fate of the artist in America. It is only later, during the First World War, that Social Credit was added to his repertoire. Then in the 1920s he takes up the theme of the causes of war and the part played by armament merchants and bankers in fomenting wars. The alarm about American culture leads to an exploration of American history and the works of Thomas Jefferson, especially his correspondence with John Adams. It is not until 1933, when the world is in the deepest throes of the Depression, that he starts writing on economics. In these pieces of writing are woven strands of his other concerns, mentioned above, and the collective force of these diatribes is quite formidable.

It is best to begin with 'Murder by Capital' written in the same year as the long pamphlet *ABC of Economics*, and originally published as an article in the *Criterion* in July 1933. 'Murder' starts by reverting to the theme of *Patria Mia* (written on his return from his first trip back to America, and first published as a series of articles in the *New Age* in 1912 before he revised them and published them in volume form in 1913, which was reissued in 1950).

> Twenty years ago, before 'one', 'we', 'the present writer' or his acquaintances had begun to think about 'cold subjects like economics' one began to notice that the social order hated *any* art of maximum intensity and preferred dilutations. The best artists were unemployed, they were unemployed long before, or at any rate appreciably before, the unemployment crisis began to make the front page in the newspapers.
>
> Capitalist society, or whatever you choose to call the social organization of 1905 to 1915 was *not* getting the most out of its available artistic 'plant'. ('Murder', *SP*, p. 227)

But he says he is angry now and in a murderous mood: 'Why should a peace-loving writer of Quaker descent be quite ready to shoot certain persons whom he has never laid eyes on?' ('Murder', *SP*, p. 228).

And again: 'I have blood lust because of what I have seen done to, and attempted against the arts in my time' ('Murder', *SP*, p. 229).

But while he did not know it in 1912, now, in 1933, he knows the cause and the solution of the problem of the social order.

> It is perhaps only now that all these disagreeable phenomena can be traced to maladministration of credit. Artists are the race's antennae. The effects of social evil show first in the arts. Most social evils are at root economic. I personally know of no social evil that cannot be cured, or very largely cured, economically.
>
> The lack of printed and exchangeable slips of paper corresponding to extant goods is at the root of bad taste, it is at the

root not of *bad* musical composition, but at the root of non-performance of the best music, ancient, modern and contemporary; it is at the root of the difficulty in printing good books *when* written. ('Murder', *SP*, p. 229)

This in essence is Pound's grievance. He has tied his youthful complaint of 1912 in with an economic analysis of the shortage of credit as the root cause of the poverty of the arts and the artists. In 'Murder', there are other minor themes such as praise for Mussolini, as I have mentioned earlier, and dislike of the arts bureaucracy. But the main causal link between artistic deprivation and credit shortage is established. The next step is to expand on the nature of money and explain why it is the root cause of so many evils.

The ABC of Economics is a long and, for Pound, a serious attempt to expound his economic philosophy. It starts by distinguishing between property, which he sees as legitimate, and capital, which he has reservations about. 'It would be possible to attack the "rights" and "privileges" of capital without attacking the rights or privileges of property' (*ABC, SP*, p. 233). This is because capital involves a claim on others and expectations of earning a return on it. He then states that the productive capacity is sufficient to afford plenty for all and the working hours could be reduced without any problem. So,

> Probably the only economic problem needing emergency solution in our time is the problem of distribution. There are enough goods, there is superabundant capacity to produce goods in superabundance. Why should anyone starve?
> (*ABC, SP*, p. 234).

In moving to the solution, Pound takes the enlightened view that money is just a token and that what it's made of – gold or paper – makes no difference. This is commonplace now but is radical for the days when the Gold Standard still had a lot of clout in economic orthodoxy.[1] The problem then is that not enough of these paper slips or tokens are around to buy up all that is produced. So he thinks one solution is to share work out among all the workers.

'It is nevertheless undeniable that if no one were allowed to work (this year 1933) more than five (5) hours a day, there would be hardly anyone out of a job and no family without paper tokens potent enough to permit them to eat' (*ABC, SP*, p. 235).

So far Pound is like many on the left and the right who in the 1930s were putting forward idealistic solutions to the problem of unemployment. The radical saw the economy as static with more workers than work. So work share seemed to be the solution, with the implicit notion that while the working day would be cut, not so the wage. Economists would say that the work sharing would also lead to wage sharing in the absence of a sudden rise in productivity. (Pound grants later in the pamphlet that even if the wage had to be cut, people currently unemployed would be better off. Of course, he does not see that those currently employed would have to take a wage cut and might well resent this.) If productivity did rise it would lead to extra output which would have to be absorbed. At this time even Keynes had not grasped the role of effective demand in the determination of employment though he was very nearly there.

Pound recognizes that cutting the length of the working day is not the whole answer. What we need is perfect money. Every good produced must be matched with a certificate of its existence, i.e., a money voucher. Pound then mentions Douglas indirectly as 'A hard-headed Scotchman' who has been criticizing the monetary system. The essence of the solution again is simply stated.

---

1 Great Britain had gone off the Gold Standard in 1931 after the fall of the Labour Government, something many in that outgoing government thought could not be done. Roosevelt upon becoming President arbitrarily changed the dollar price of gold, thus devaluing the dollar. Ezra Pound makes no mention of either of these events at this stage which he should have welcomed. Later he criticized Roosevelt for raising the price of gold as a concession to the Rothschilds.

Call it a dollar, or a quid or ten shillings or anything else you like. If a quid is a certificate of work done (goods produced) and you produce twice as much as you did yesterday, you have either got to have more quids OR you have got to agree, all of you, that the quid that meant one bushel now means two bushels. That is to say if you, in any sense, mean to play fair. (*ABC, SP*, p. 236–7)

Or, as economists would say, prices have to be completely flexible. Of course the problem then was that some prices – of agricultural products, say – were flexible while other prices – of manufactured products – and wages of industrial workers were relatively rigid. Or as Pound expresses it, '. . . if money is scarce and an ox sells at four pence you can conceivably have economic justice at four pence per ox. But you cannot have social justice at four pence per *ox* and ten shillings per beefsteak' (*ABC*, SP, p. 236–7).

However, changes in the price level – whether inflation or deflation – are controlled in 'a dark room back of a bank, hung with deep purple curtains'. So, 'Who, my brother, controlleth the bank?' Of course in Britain a private bank – the Bank of England – controls money, while in America, control has passed into non-democratic hands. Pound does not mention the Federal Reserve or its constitution but just assumes that it is controlled not in the public interest. The shortage of money as it is currently controlled then leads to an exposition of Major Douglas's theory.

Douglas's theory is so central to Pound's economics that it requires a detour from our exposition of *ABC*. Major Douglas argued in his pamphlet *Economic Democracy*, and in subsequent writings, that there was a simple explanation for the persistence of unemployment and poverty amidst plenty. *Economic Democracy* is about much more than what Douglas became famous for. It is a powerful argument for decentralization and for devolution of economic powers. But what got through was Douglas's criticism of the economic system. The key according to him was the structure of costs and prices as decided by accountants and bankers. His argument was that there was a permanent structural problem in the way goods were costed and priced. At each stage, the gross cost of output – raw materials used plus wages plus profits – exceeded the income generated, which was only the wages and profits. Thus the sum of gross costs exceeded the sum of net 'value added' as we would call it today. This gap, according to Douglas, was the measure of the extra credit needed – the credit that was not being supplied. He called it his A + B theorem. It is worth quoting in full.

> Payments may be divided into two groups: Group A – All payments made to individuals (wages, salaries and dividends). Group B – All payments made to other organizations (raw materials, bank charges, and other external costs). Now the rate of flow of purchasing power to individuals is represented by A, but since all payments go into prices the rate of flow of prices cannot be less than A + B. The product of any factory may be considered as something which the public ought to be able to buy, although in many cases it is an intermediate product of no use to individuals, but only to subsequent manufacture; but since A will not purchase A + B, a proportion of the product at least equivalent to B must be distributed by some form of purchasing power which is not comprised in the descriptions under A. It will be necessary at a later stage to show that this additional purchasing power is provided by loan credits (bank overdrafts) or export credit. (Douglas, p. 22)

As it happens, this is a simple fallacy. The problem is that counting in raw material purchased at each stage amounts to double counting since when they were sold the income they generated had been already distributed. By the time B payments are made they correspond to A payments of an earlier stage of production. No new income need be generated corresponding to the materials purchased. Douglas almost sees this when he mentions intermediate products above. Today the distinction between the gross value of output and the value added is familiar as the basis of Value Added Tax. If Douglas had not exaggerated the importance of this miscalculation by calling it his A + B theorem, he would have saved himself much criticism.

But his appeal was not diminished by that. Douglas became a hit with the political and social crowd that hangs around at Speakers' Corners and joins any march or demonstration. He had of course hoped that he was offering the middle way between the orthodox way and the extremist left. But he attracted the fringes of the left and the right-wing anarchists, Catholic reformers and Tory money cranks. Famous names such as Hilaire Belloc, G. K. Chesterton, Herbert Read, T. E. Hulme and, of course, A. R. Orage were attracted to his camp. For a while between 1920 and 1936, Douglas and his Social Credit movement were a big noise among the restless and the agitated. It all died down once Keynes's *General Theory of Employment, Interest and Money* provided the answer that took the mystery out of the problem of shortage of effective demand. Once that happened Douglas's star waned and it was only in Canada that a Social Credit Party survived (Finlay, 1972). But that is another story altogether.

Douglas's followers were mesmerized by the 'theorem' as often happens with quack cures. Douglas himself resisted the criticism by saying, somewhat mystifyingly, 'Let not the patient reader allow himself to become confused by the fact that B has at some previous time been represented by payments of wages, salaries and dividends. While this is of course true it is irrelevant – it is the rate of flow which is vital' (Douglas, pp. 24–5). This remark obscures the simple fallacy but does not remove it. Whether an economy is growing or shrinking, i.e. whatever the rate of flow, will make little difference to the fallacy. As one gets nearer to the final consumable output, the B payments are a multiple of the A payments and the growth rate of the economy will not much affect this disproportion.

The only thing one can salvage from all of Douglas's analysis is what Keynes said about his A + B theorem in his *General Theory* (*GT* hereafter). This is that one can ignore raw material usage as it involves double counting. But if money has been set aside according to accounting conventions for amortization but no investment corresponds to such funds either within the firm or in the economy at large there will be a shortfall of effective demand. This shortfall will hang much more on a shrinking economy than a growing one.

The brilliant LSE economist and Labour Party intellectual Evan Durbin pointed this out at about the time Pound was writing his pamphlet, by setting up what we now call an input-output table and showing the mistake Douglas was making. Durbin was at that time using a schema F. A. Hayek had used in his 1931 lectures at the London School of Economics, which became the book *Prices and Production*. Hayek also sought an explanation for the trade cycle but his reasoning was different from that of Douglas. Hayek subsequently became prominent as an anti-Keynesian in his economics and a libertarian in his political philosophy. But in the 1930s, Hayek was part of the orthodoxy which resisted any reflation and wanted the cycle of unemployment to take its course, no matter how long that was, so that prices and wages could fall to the level which could restore full employment. The Hayek association led many defenders of Douglas to dismiss the Durbin critique. John Finlay, who wrote a book on Social Credit in 1972, dismisses Durbin lightly but is not aware that what Durbin said is now almost the first lesson of Introductory Economics about the circular flow of income.[2]

Douglas advocated issuing enough credit to make up for the shortfall, which would be the sum of B payments. But he made this

2 Hugh Gaitskell, who later became Leader of the Labour Party and was a friend of Durbin, cites Durbin's analysis in his critique of Douglas: see Gaitskell, H. T. N. 'Four Monetary Heretics' (1933) in Cole, G. D. H., *What Everybody Wants To Know About Money* (1933), pp. 346–413. Finlay, John *Social Credit: The English Origins* (1972), pp. 110–11.

into a scheme whereby firms would price goods below cost and then be issued Treasury certificates redeemable in money. This was unnecessary bureaucracy. The essence of the scheme is a subsidy compensating producers for the amount of B payments. These subsidies were the Social Credit. Since banks may resist giving out such credit, it would require the nationalization of money supply and credit to make it work.

Isolated in Rapallo, Pound does not seem to have been aware of the debate raging about Douglas's views in Britain, where left-wing parties – Communist and Labour especially – made his theories a subject of constant attack. Keynes, who had one foot inside the Establishment and one firmly outside, described Douglas as belonging to 'the underworlds' of economics along with Karl Marx and Silvio Gesell for having wrestled with 'the great puzzle of effective demand' (*GT*, p. 32). He goes on to say:

> The strength of Major Douglas's advocacy has, of course, largely depended on orthodoxy having no valid reply to much of his destructive criticism . . . Major Douglas is entitled to claim as against some of his orthodox adversaries, that he at least has not been wholly oblivious of the outstanding problem of our economic system. Yet he has scarcely established an equal claim to rank – a private, perhaps, but not a major in the brave army of heretics – with Mandeville, Malthus, Gesell and Hobson, who, following their intuitions, have preferred to see the truth obscurely and imperfectly rather than to maintain error, reached indeed with clearness and consistency and by easy logic but on hypotheses inappropriate to the facts.
> (*GT*, pp. 370–1)

To return to *ABC*, Pound starts Part Three of the pamphlet with Douglas's argument. Having outlined it as I have done above, he draws the following four conclusions which are very much his own.

The requirements so far on our list are:

1. 'Money' as certificate of work done.
2. 'Work done' to be in a sense 'inside the system', that is to say, it must be 'necessary' or at any rate it must be work that someone WANTS done. The product must be what someone lacks – I lack half a loaf of bread daily or thereabouts. I lack a few suits of clothes per annum, etc.
3. There must be some way for everyone to get enough money or common-carrier to satisfy a reasonable number of lacks . . . The simplest road is *via* work, and I suspect any other . . .
4. Fairness in the issuance of certificates. (I think the various Douglas plans fall mainly under this heading).
(*ABC, SP*, pp. 242–3)

It is fair to comment that Pound is here in a long tradition of utopian writers who treat the economy as if it were an inert system to be fashioned at will. Thus the idea of money based on work was put forward by the French anarchist Proudhon who was taken to task by Marx. The problem with work money is that one hour of a labourer's time is not the same as one hour of a surgeon's time. How many 'certificates' are we to issue for one as against the other, and who is to decide? In a market economy the wages and salaries of workers of different skills are determined by supply and demand, albeit within the context of institutional arrangements such as trade unions. But the idealist does not like the market arrangement of wages.

What Pound calls lack is what economists call need, but what the market reacts to is wants backed up by purchasing power. Who is to decide whether Mr Pound's lack of a few suits per annum is more urgent than the need of a family for children's clothes? The market decides in a rough and ready way by assuming that certain skills earn so much in wages, which determines the household's income from which it finances purchases. But more than that, if money only matched the wage bill, how would one finance investment for replacing old capital and for new investment? Utopian economics is not easier but more demanding than traditional economics.

But to resume Pound's exposition, he begins a discussion of the distinction between time and money and asserts the primacy of non-market, unpaid work and how leisure, if free of worry, can contribute to happiness. This takes him without any clear logical connection into Jefferson and Van Buren, though at this stage Jefferson's objections to banks are not mentioned. But the issue of carefree leisure as against forced idleness brings Pound back to the suggestion of shorter working days. He recognizes, however, that 'You can't arouse any very fiery passion on the bare plea of less work. It spells less pay to most hearers.'

So the remedy is 'By simple extensions of credit (paper credit) it would be possible to leave the nominal pay exactly where it is, but it requires an almost transcendent comprehension of credit to understand this' (*ABC, SP,* p. 244). Pound ultimately does not believe a shorter working day will sell as against higher nominal pay.

He then gets into the byways of Free Trade and then Malthus and the need for population control – another nostrum for reducing unemployment that used to be advanced. Pound has little time for this but his despair for America keeps on breaking through in odd places throughout this essay. Thus:

> Give a people an almost perfect government, and in two generations they will let it rot from sheer laziness (*vide* the USA where not one person in ten exercises his rights and not one person in ten thousand has the faintest idea of the aims and ambitions of the country's great founders and lawmakers. Their dung has covered their heads). (*ABC, SP,* pp. 245–6)

The economic solution is clear but its implementation remains a problem of politics.

'Economics is concerned with what should be done, not with how you are going to get a controlling group of men to carry out an idea; but with the idea, with the proper equations.' But 'Science or no science an economic system or lack of system is bound to be affected by the political system in which or besides which it exists, and more especially by the preconceptions or prejudices or predispositions and attitudes implied in the political system' (*ABC*, SP, pp. 246–7). Having now arrived at politics, in Part 4, Pound begins to mention Jefferson and his elitist democratic ideas with some approval. At the birth of a nation, 'any new governing class is bound to be composed of exceptional men, or at any rate of men having more energy and being therefore more fit (apt) to govern than their fellows.' These 'best men, kaloikagathoi' were present in the days of Jefferson and Adams though there were differences among these leaders. Usually one cannot rely on the elite to show such responsibility. This then leads to Mussolini and his leadership. 'The point is that the orders of an omniscient despot and of an intelligent democracy would be very much alike in so far as they affected the main body of the country's economics' (*ABC*, SP, p. 248).

I am imposing a greater sense of order on the essay than would be obvious to a new reader arriving at it afresh. This is because it makes sense in the total context of Pound's thought and also after a while one gets used to the rambling style where the author suddenly goes off on a tangent or puts in some (to this reader at least) obscure historical reference. What follows the passage quoted above is rather like that where Pound gets back to the distinction between property and capital, the durability of credit systems with remarks about heathens trading glass beads and Mantuans creating a cloth pool as a stabilizing device for cloth makers, etc.

But then Pound returns to the main theme again and reiterates the four points he had made before about work certificates. This is the section entitled 'In 1933 Where Are We?'

> Make fair the distribution of paper slips certifying work done, keep the work distributed among a sufficient proportion of the people, and you still must have constant caginess not to find yourself in October with nothing but wheat, or nothing but aluminium frying pans . . . And towards this end, there is probably no equation other than the greatest watchfulness of the greatest number of the most competent.
> (*ABC, SP,* p. 249)

As in all utopian economics, one has to rely on the brightest and the best to rule with wisdom so as not to be flooded with aluminium pans in October. But then who is actually in charge anyway? The banks control the credit and 'use their freedom to inflate and deflate to their own disproportionate advantage'. Nations ought to control their credit systems.

The USA according to Pound was in control of its credit system until the days of Martin Van Buren but lost it after the Civil War. (As I explained above, this refers to the Jackson-Biddle battle and the way Van Buren took the gold stock back under Federal control. I shall return to this theme later since it requires delving into the Adams–Jefferson letters.) But then again Pound retracts: 'Once again we are not even concerned with HOW a people or nation is to get control of its economics but with WHAT it ought to do with them if it did get control' (*ABC, SP*, p. 249). So again the issue is that adequate amounts of slips should be made available to everyone even if the distribution is not totally just, i.e., a minimum income for all matters more than equal income for all. 'Once a human being is comfortable, without actual suffering and free, more or less, from IMMEDIATE worry, he will not bother (to an almost incredible degree he will refuse to bother) about economics' (*ABC, SP*, p. 250).

Thus Pound arrives at what even today is the radical proposal of a national dividend or a Citizen's Income given as of right, much as the franchise.[3] He would like the recipient citizen to perform some task in return for the dividend. He remains sceptical that issuing the dividends alone would solve the question of what is to be produced and how – i.e., he sees the general problem of planning in an economy. Yet his main concern, to which he keeps on coming back, is that adequate amount of credit should be available. Given the behaviour of the banks which he again states, his conclusion is inevitable: 'I take it that in the perfect economic state the cost of money is reduced to nothing, to something like the mere cost of postage, and that this cost is borne by the state, i.e. distributed so as to be a burden on no one in particular' (*ABC, SP*, p. 254).

This runs pretty close to Keynes's own conclusion about the necessity of bringing the nominal interest rate down as low as would be tolerated by the bond market. The 'euthanasia of the rentier' is what Keynes thought would permanently alleviate the problem of effective demand. The world has not quite worked out like that. But for much of the post-1945 period governments did issue interest-free debt – i.e. currency to provide full employment. It is only when the ensuing inflation got out of hand that orthodoxy reasserted itself. But hyperinflation or even mild inflation was far from the minds of Pound and other reformers in the 1930s.

In the years after the Second World War, governments took over the control of the money supply. The Gold Standard was abandoned in national monetary systems, though a mild version of it lasted in international payments under the Bretton Woods system till 1971. It is difficult to imagine how different the present world is from the interwar period. Much of what Pound was agitating for about provision of work was made possible by Keynes's revolutionary work. The governments stood ready via fiscal policy – taxes

3 The literature on citizens' income is very large. See, among others, Desai, Meghnad, 'A Basic Income Proposal' (1998) in Skidelsky, Robert, et al., *The State of the Future*, 1998. Also Van Parijs, Philippe, *Real Freedom for All: What (If Anything) Can Justify Capitalism?* (1995).

and expenditures – plus any deficit financing, funded often by printing money, to assure full employment. This period – the so-called Golden Age of Keynesianism – lasted for twenty-five years from the late 1940s to the early 1970s. But even today while governments are chary of issuing interest-free debt – printing money, in other words – they still acknowledge the responsibility of sustaining high and stable levels of employment, albeit with a wary eye on inflation. One could agree with Pound when he says, 'The state conceived as the public convenience. Money conceived as a public convenience. Neither as private bonanza' (*ABC, SP*, p. 254).

Pound then moves on to a view of economics which is nowadays associated with the Green or Alternative Economics. He asserts that wealth consists of reproducible (i.e., animal and vegetable) products. Manufacturing cannot increase and multiply by itself. 'Half the modern trouble is the mania or hallucination or *idée fixe* of MARKET and market value.' This is because 'The primitive grazer counts his property in sheep and is not continually worried if he cannot sell out his whole breed.'

What follows is surprising in view of the usury ban. Rather than argue that money is barren and so should not bear interest, Pound argues that the basis of interest payments is in the natural tendency of plants and animals to multiply.

> The practices of rent and interest arise out of the natural disposition of grain and animals to multiply. The sense of right and justice which has sustained the main practice of rent and interest through the ages, *despite* countless instances of particular injustice in the application, is inherent in the nature of animal and vegetables. (*ABC, SP*, p. 256)

What is remarkable about that pair of sentences is not that they are sensible but that the good sense in them is not sustained. If the origin of interest is in the productivity of Nature, then there is nothing artificial about charging it. If money is invested in animal husbandry or grain cultivation, interest is chargeable. But, as any economist would point out, once you have an interest in one part of the economy, it is hard to keep it out from anywhere else. That is what economists call the tendency to equilibrium. There may be small differences in the level of the rate of interest and occasionally, and at the cost of surveillance and enforcement, you may forbid charging from an isolated sector, but a general ban is unsustainable.

The next step in the argument is one close to Pound's heart. This is the doctrine of property as expounded by Jefferson, or at least Jefferson as read by Pound: 'The two extremes: superstitious sacrosanctity of "property" *versus* Jefferson's "The Earth belongs to the living", which was part dogma, and part observation of a fact so obvious that it took a man of genius to perceive it.'

The following step may not be obviously logical to all, but forms the heart of Pound's battle against debt and banking.

> It led Jefferson to the belief that no nation has the right to contract debts not payable within the lifetime of the contractors, which he interpreted to mean the lifetime of the majority of the contractors who were of age at the date of contract. So that from a first estimate of thirty-five years, he finally fixed on nineteen years as the limit of validity of such debts.
> (*ABC, SP*, p. 256)

What Jefferson said about debt in the late eighteenth century became for Pound the guiding truth for his own day. Much of American financial history is then caricatured in terms of decline from the Jeffersonian Golden Dictum. From Jefferson through Jackson and Van Buren, the struggle of the agrarian interest against the banks succeeds in restraining financial power.

'By the light of his [Jefferson's] intelligence American economics improved from the time of the revolution till the confusion of the US civil war.' Pound ignores the obvious fact that if, since his departure from the USA in 1908, his father was able to send him money painlessly, it was thanks to Alexander Hamilton's shrewdness in establishing a bank over the opposition of Jefferson and his Party. If the USA did not remain an agricultural backwater like Argentina but became a manufacturing and financial powerhouse, it was thanks to Hamilton and his financial acumen. But like many romantic nostalgics, Pound would have none of it, championing Jefferson against Hamilton in the perennial debate of American history.

Pound knows of course that the modern economy no longer relies on animal power for production. But his conclusion from that is that work could be cut down.

> It is as idiotic to expect members of a civilized twentieth-century community to go on working eight hours a day as it would be to expect the shepherd to try to grow wool on his sheep by hand; the farmer to blow with his own breath on each buried seed to warm it; the poulterer to sit on his hens' eggs.
> (*ABC, SP*, p. 257)

The fifth and last part is entitled 'Minor Addenda and Varia'. Here Pound says tolerant things about stock-market speculators – all right as long as what they do does not impact on 'the food and welfare' of ordinary people. He then disclaims any novelty in his arguments and quotes David Hume as saying similar things. Yet he attributes to Hume, albeit indirectly, the following: 'You will probably find nothing more valid inside its own scope than the statement that prosperity depends not on the quantity of money in a country but on its *constantly increasing*.'

This is a surprising reading of Hume, who, while he did say that infusion of money into an economy could increase real activity, also recognized that there were limits to this process and pure inflation could eventually occur. But again, in the context of the Depression and given that the monetary authorities in the USA were at fault in restricting the money supply as the pre-eminent monetarist Milton Friedman has argued, Pound is not too far off the mark in his advocacy of inflation.

> There are four elements; and it is useless trying to function with three:
> 1. The product.
> 2. The want.
> 3. The means of transport.
> 4. AND the certificates of value, preferably legal tender and 'general', in the sense that they should be good for wheat, iron, lumber, dress goods, or whatever the heart and stomach desire. (*ABC*, *SP*, p. 260)

How this would be achieved depends on who controls the money supply – the certificates of value. 'The best system of government, economically speaking, is that which best balances the four elements listed above, be it republic, monarchy, or soviet or dictatorship.'

Which brings him to Italy's premier: 'Mussolini as intelligent man is more interesting than Mussolini as the Big Stick. The Duce's aphorisms and perceptions can be studied apart from his means of getting them into action.'

In the Finale, Pound makes an attack on Keynes. He begins by citing a remark of Orage – which he describes as 'an expression simple enough to be understood by almost anyone, save possibly Maynard Keynes or some paid mouthpiece of British Liberalism'.

> Would you call it inflation [Orage had written] to issue tickets for every seat in a hall, despite the fact that the hall has never before been filled, or more than a fourth of the seats sold, because of there not being enough tickets available?
> Inflation would consist in issuing more tickets than there are seats. ('R.H.C.' [Orage], *New English Weekly*, 16 June 1932; quoted by Pound, *SP*, p. 262)

Pound calls this 'the foundation stone of the New (Douglas) economics'. His swipe at Keynes that follows is ironic in the light of how Keynes's insights displaced Douglas permanently.

> Keynes may have found it out by now; he was incapable of understanding it in 1920, and until he makes definite public acknowledgement of the value of C. H. Douglas, I shall be compelled either to regard him as a saphead or to believe that his writings arise from motives lying deeper in the hinterland of his consciousness than courtesy can permit to penetrate.
> (*ABC, SP*, p. 262)

Keynes was in fact to acknowledge Douglas, but as I quoted above only as a private in the battle against classical economics. Keynes was able to be rather snooty about Douglas because he had the confidence that his theory was better than anyone else's. Pound does not seem to have read *The General Theory* when it came out in 1936, as indeed he did not acknowledge much else that was happening on the New Deal front that he should have approved of. He just stuck by Douglas.

Finally we come to 'Conclusions: Or a Postscript in the Spring'. Pound introduces yet another of his favourite themes: 'An economic system in which it is more profitable to make guns to blow men to pieces than to grow grain or make useful machinery, is an outrage, and its supporters are enemies of the race' (*ABC, SP*, p. 263).

Pound then rounds up his solution for the economy by the even more radical suggestion that if the government is going to print money – certificates of value for payment of work done for it in the public sector – then taxation is unnecessary. Public employment could be financed by printing new money. Indeed, one could go beyond that. Thus the government need not tax at all but just print money to finance all expenditure. Not even the most libertarian group had advocated this, but it is an idea worth exploring rather than dismissing as a recipe for hyperinflation.

Pound ends by urging the establishment of a new Material Party with three parts to its platform:

1. When enough exists, means should be found to distribute it to the people who need it.
2. It is the business of the nation to see that its own citizens get their share, before worrying about the rest of the world. (If not, what is the sense of being 'united' or organized as a state? What is the meaning of 'citizen'?)
3. When the potential production (the possible production) of anything is sufficient to meet everyone's needs, it is the business of the governments to see that both production *and* distribution are achieved. (*ABC, SP*, p. 264)

This concludes *ABC*. I have dwelt on it at some length because it is the first and the longest of Pound's essays on economics. It brings together virtually all the themes he was to repeat in later pamphlets. But it is remarkable for the absence of one trait. It is entirely free of Jew-baiting, of his virulent anti-Semitism. It is thus possible to separate his economics from his anti-Semitism. At this stage in the winter and spring of 1933, Pound is a radical reformer interested in full employment which he hopes would be achieved by means of a monetary policy which is designed to provide enough money to employ everyone. The policy aim is what we would now call Keynesian. The analysis is Douglas plus a generous dollop of Pound himself. It is not cranky or crazy but quite restrained, although it lacks the elegance of a fully worked-out economic theory. While Keynes was not yet ready with his full-blown theory, which he presented in *The General Theory*, he was already lecturing the newly elected US President on 'The Means to Prosperity'.[4] He

---

4 'The Means to Prosperity' was written in March 1933 for *The Times* with a special extra section for the American edition on the multiplier reprinted from the *New Statesman and Nation*. The American version is reproduced in *The Collected Writings of John Maynard Keynes Vol. IX: Essays in Persuasion*, pp. 335–66.

had grasped the essence of the solution. Pound does not seem to be aware of what Keynes was writing, or, if he is, he certainly does not refer to it. His mind was made up on Keynes as it was on several other matters. Over the next dozen years as he wrote more on economics, Pound appears to take no notice of Keynes.

I shall go through Pound's pamphlets more or less chronologically, noting the themes as they are addressed but only go into detail if they are significantly different from what we have already seen. 'Social Credit: An Impact' written in 1935, is more bitty and abusive comments about Jews and bankers have begun to creep in, but much of what he wrote in *ABC* is repeated here. There is a recurring chant of *Work is not a commodity, Money is not a commodity* throughout the pamphlet. There is also, however, a greater sense of despair.

> The English are degrading their empire, murdering their home population for the sake of a fixed idea as to the nature of money.
>
> The American New Deal to date (December 1934–January 1935) has shown no comprehension of fundamentals, no perception of the basic relations of currency system, credit system to the needs and purchasing power of the whole people.
> ('SC', 1951, pp. 6–7)

This is somewhat strange because by 1935 Britain had gone off the Gold Standard and the rate of interest had fallen to 2 per cent. Indeed, there was a revival in British economic activity much before it happened in other developed countries. Unemployment in terms of the percentage of insured workers (the best measure available for the interwar period), had fallen from 22 per cent in 1932 to 15.5 per cent in 1935, while the wage rate remained stable. In the USA, the New Deal had started with a banking holiday and hearings about banks by the US Congress, which was shaking up the bankers. By December 1934, the money stock was higher by 20 per cent over its level in March 1933. Unemployment in the USA had come down from 12.6 million in 1933 to 10.2 million – by around a sixth. Hourly earnings had risen based on an index 1931 = 100 from 87 in 1933 to 107 by 1935.[5]

Friedman and Schwartz as historians of the US monetary system accord a big role to the New Deal in the transformation of the American banking system. It is worth quoting them at some length since Ezra Pound went on asserting for a long time afterwards that nothing had got better under the New Deal. Friedman and Schwartz say of the New Deal:

> [T]he collapse of the banking system produced a demand for remedial legislation that led to the enactment of federal deposit insurance, to changes in the powers of the Federal Reserve System, and to closer regulation of banks and other financial institutions. The depressed state of the economy, the large preceding fall in prices and, despite these conditions, the poor competitive position of our exports thanks to the depreciation of the pound and other currencies, all combined with the New Deal atmosphere to foster experimentation with the monetary standard. The experiments involved temporary departure from gold, a period of flexible and depreciating exchange rates, silver purchases, subsequent nominal return to gold at a higher price for gold, and drastic changes in the terms and conditions under which gold could be held and obtained by private parties. (Friedman and Schwartz, p. 420)

Given that Pound was obsessed with banks and bankers at this time (the celebrated Cantos XLII–LI were written at this time and relate to banking and usury), it is surprising that he did not register the upheaval in US banking. Since he was at this time actively

---

5 Data on UK and US employment and wages from Chick, V., *On Money, Method and Keynes* (1992), Table 1.1, where the sources are cited. For money-supply data for the US, Friedman, M. and A. Schwartz, *A Monetary History of the United States 1867–1960* (1963), Table 15, p. 430–1.

in correspondence with many Americans including the President and the distinguished Yale economist Irving Fisher, we cannot say he was not informed. He just does not seem to have been able to see anything that did not exactly fit his own preconceptions. Otherwise there is no explanation either for his persistence in repeating what he had said in 1933 or for the rising tone of despair and violence, evident for example in the anti-bankers diatribe he launches himself into in this pamphlet.

> This situation is the glory and boast of Messrs Norman and Rothschild. It is the certificate of efficiency. Deterding, Herbert Lawrence, Duff Cooper, Sarvazy, Sieff, De Wendel, Robert Protot, the brothers Schneider of Creusot, and ten thousand fatted bankers proclaim the virtues of 'orthodox' economics, assisted by 500 cuts, and titled straw men, waiting for something to break. ('SC', p. 10-11)

Beyond that, he despairs of other European countries as well. Thus he is not pleased with what is happening in Germany: 'Schacht, the prize tailor's dummy, has gone out with a begging box, to stimulate Xmas spirit. The dregs of German farce comedy can attain no deeper bathos.'

The people mentioned in these outbursts are a bit puzzling – some of the names are today not known although they might have carried some importance at the time; others we do still know of today but it is unclear as to why they are in his list. Unsurprising are Norman – Montagu Norman, then Governor of the Bank of England – and Rothschild. But why Duff Cooper, who was just a hanger-on in politics? Pound's dismissal of Schacht is also surprising since by 1935, German economic policy had succeeded in lowering unemployment quite sharply and had been following a policy of low interest rates.[6]

6 On Nazi economic policy in this period see Overy, Richard, *War and Economy in the Third Reich* (1994); see also Desai, Meghnad, *Marx's Revenge* (2002), chapter 10.

There is also a detour about the history of Italian banking. Pound regarded the Monte dei Paschi of Siena to be an ideal bank since at a time of distress Cosimo de Medici gave an advance against some grazing lands and grazing rights. Since this showed faith in Nature's reproductive powers, Pound regards him as a soundly based banker. Against this, there is contrasted the 'hell bank', Banca San Giorgio of Genoa, which goes on aggrandizing to itself various taxation powers of the commune of Genoa. The stories are followed up in the parallel Cantos. Having grounded himself in this contrast, Pound fails to adjust his ideas to other banks which have been long-lasting and successful – the House of Rothschild for example. But in general he distrusts debt without realizing that debt is just a way of readjusting the flow of income to match the flow of expenditure. Debt is borrowing against future income. Why it should cause such devastation to all productive life as Pound laments in Canto XLV is not clear.

> with usura, sin against nature,
> is thy bread ever more of stale rags
> is thy bread dry as paper,
> with no mountain wheat, no strong flour . . .
>
> . . . wool comes not to market
> sheep bringeth no grain with usura . . .
>
> Usura rusteth the chisel
> It rusteth the craft and the craftsman
> It gnaweth the thread in the loom . . .

Much of modern life, indeed even what his parents would have enjoyed by way of houses (which gives the lie to this poem's first line, 'With usura hath no man a house of good stone'), would have been financed by debt. Municipalities or national governments have built roads and bridges and viaducts and tramways and waterworks in towns and countryside by floating debt.

Even painters and sculptors have had bankers as patrons, in Amsterdam, London and New York but also in Pound's favourite country, Italy, through its glorious centuries of painting. To say as he does in Canto XLV,

> with usura
> hath no man a painted paradise on his church wall ...

is just false: bankers were commissioning such paintings, and were painted as characters in them, through the centuries. But Pound had a bee in his bonnet about usury, and a passionate denunciation makes better poetry than an effort to be reasonable.

Ignoring the abuse directed at Jews and bankers, there are two new ideas in 'SC', both derived from Douglas but not mentioned in *ABC* – 'the increment of association' and 'the cultural heritage'. The increment of association is what economists call economies of size, for example, ten people together may accomplish more than ten separately. Cultural heritage refers to the stock of knowledge, inventions and so on. These two ideas are mentioned just baldly without any elaboration, but the point is that money issuance as Douglas prescribes will lead not to inflation but to higher real product because of the increment of association.

Pound also airs his quick and easy history of American financial developments, best quoted in full:

> For a hundred years states have done little with their credit save sabotage it, save use it for less than its value, pay private companies tribute. A government of hypnotized rabbits could not behave with greater imbecility, and there can, in the long run, be no greater treason to the people.
>
> All this is known, all this has been known ten times over. It was known to Jackson and Van Buren. The American Civil War shelved the knowledge. Not only did the American pay with their blood (a million dead), for negro freedom, but they paid with the death of knowledge. America paid by her loss of

> memory, she came out of her Civil War with unspeakable shell-shock, and a dead loss of cultural heritage of which she was utterly and unspeakably unconscious. The war of the 1830s is not to be found in the school books. Jackson is regarded as a tobacco-chewing half-wit, or a tuppeny militarist, the murderer of a few Indians, and the victor of New Orleans. Van Buren either vilified or forgotten. Only abnormal Englishmen have ever heard of such presidents. ('SC', pp. 11–12)

This particular lament, with the addition of a Jefferson-Adams chapter, recurs through the various essays and of course in the Cantos XXXI–XLI. Here again, as in many other of his opinions, Pound echoes a well-worn tradition of monetary cranks. Jefferson against Hamilton, the agrarian versus the commercial, the Augustan sage against the bastard upstart, the American patriot and Republican against the partisan of the English – these tropes are present even today, as can be seen by reading Gore Vidal. The puzzle about Pound is that he is a modernist in his poetry and until the end of the First World War identified with the Future and against all old-fashioned forces. Then suddenly in the space of twenty years, we see him defending late-eighteenth-century agrarian capitalism and practically everything American from before the Civil War. This might be yet another way in which Pound the exile coped with his deeply felt rejection, turning away from the America that he felt had cast him off and embracing its lost past.

It is in the next major essay, an article rather than a pamphlet, 'The Individual in his Milieu', that Pound adds the next big plank to his economic programme. This is his endorsement of the ideas of Silvio Gesell, an economist whom Keynes noted with approbation in his *General Theory*. Gesell's scheme of stamped money was designed to discourage the hoarding of money instead of spending it: money, he proposed, should lose value as time passed after its printing, which would speed up spending. Keynes had attributed the demand for money hoards to liquidity preference. He said that people demanded interest to give up their liquidity and that this reluctance to give up cash hoards might set a lower barrier to interest rates. Now, if at specified periods after money is printed, it has to be stamped, at a cost, in order that it should retain its value, holding on to money becomes costly. It is as if money earned a negative interest rate if not spent. This idea appealed much when during the Depression, underspending was the main danger. As Pound puts it in this essay, 'Gesell *invented* counter-usury.'

He opens with an opaque incursion into the history of usury. Again, some names are mentioned that mean little to the reader – Claudius Salmasius, Gabriel Biel, Francisco Curtio, et al. When he comes to Gesell, Pound declares that he is interested in 'the utility and vitality' of his thought as a supplement to Douglas in solving the problem at hand.

> Gesell questioned the privilege of money over and above all other products of human ingenuity, and he declared against its being the sole fabrication free of tax in a world wherein the good life was being, with increasing acrimony, taxed and stifled out of existence. He, thereupon, devised a tax on money, which requires no bureaucracy to levy it, and which falls with utter impartial justice on every hoarder or delayer of money.
> ('Individual', *SP*, p. 275)

Pound is also pleased that Gesell's scheme was adopted in the Tyrolean border town of Woergl (or Wörgl) and in the Bavarian town of Lilienthal. Pound says that in Woergl (a name that recurs in Pound's monetary essays), the tax was 1 per cent per month which is rather high, while Gesell himself had proposed a tax of 1 *mil* per week or 5.2 per cent per year according to Keynes. Pound does not refer to Gesell's proposal of nationalizing land so that rent could be abolished, or interest rates being driven down to zero by his stamp scheme. The zero-rent idea was derived from Henry George who believed that a single tax on the monopoly privileges of land ownership would be sufficient to meet all fiscal needs.

Keynes pays a handsome tribute to Gesell; a tribute much more generous than what he has to say about Douglas. Indeed Keynes gets quite carried away in his assessment of Gesell's book, *The Natural Economic Order*:

> The purpose of the book as a whole may be described as the establishment of an anti-Marxian socialism, a reaction against *laissez-faire* built on theoretical foundations totally unlike those of Marx in being based on a repudiation instead of an acceptance of the classical hypotheses, and on an unfettering of competition instead of its abolition. I believe that the future will learn more from the spirit of Gesell than from that of Marx. (*GT*, Chapter 23)

Keynes's hope for Gesell as an answer to Marx remains to be fulfilled. But as a minor writer of the interwar period he was useful to Pound.

Elsewhere in his essay Pound again attacks German policy under Schacht:

> Germany under the heel of Dr Schacht (no better than William or Von Papen) has suppressed all her *Freiwirtschaft* organizations and deserves whatever she gets. This is her own crime against herself and goes to augment the long list of high commercial treasons committed by Germans since 1919 against their own fatherland.

But Italy under Mussolini is doing very well.

> At the date of writing this article, 3 June 1935, the official Italian publications contain more honesty and intelligence than all the other government publications in Europe and America put together. A will towards truth, towards the good of the people, must, if enlightened, take count of possibility *in* space and time, that is in a particular time and in a particular area, amid given material circumstance. At the present moment no

other major government has any such will whatsoever.

Germany is most enslaved, France most befuddled, and neither England nor America inspire a hog's worth of respect outside their own publics hypnotized by news control and perverted publicity. (23 April 1935, anno XIII, tredici.)

Still fairly free of anti-Semitic prejudice economically, politically Pound is completely sold on Italy and against Anglo-American politics. His stance on Germany remains hostile, however, so clearly he is not yet in favour of Hitler as he was to be later.

It is the condition of America and to some extent Britain that concerns Pound throughout these writings. At this stage in the 1930s he was in constant correspondence with Senators and Representatives, economists and other academics. He was part of an anti-Roosevelt coalition built up around the journal *American Review* edited by the wealthy publisher Seward Collins. Round Collins, there gathered neo-Thomists and Southern Agrarians who admired Jefferson, and English Distributists like Hilaire Belloc and Chesterton, who admired medieval England and criticized the 'servile state'. Many of these were money cranks and more often than not anti-Semitic.

Pound's concern was to push his stamp scrip scheme, arguing for social credit. He failed to see that some of the things he wanted were in fact happening although in a more conventional guise than the drastic changes that he was calling for. We now see how radical the New Deal was and how at the same time it preserved America as a liberal capitalist democracy. However, at the time Roosevelt was attracting much criticism from left and right.[7]

7 Schlesinger, Arthur, *The Age of Roosevelt*, Volume 3: *The Politics of Upheaval* (1958) describes some of these criticisms in detail. See especially Chapter 1 'The Theology of Ferment'. Schlesinger (p. 73) says of Pound's attack on Roosevelt: 'Pound turned his back on his native land (though in 1934 he struck up a correspondence with William Dudley Pelly's Silver Shirts), denounced Franklin D. Roosevelt and "the Nude eel", and settled down in Rapallo to enjoy the Second Coming of the gentle Christ.'

Pound could not bear Roosevelt and his policies. This is blind prejudice since Roosevelt came nearest to implementing the sort of changes Pound wanted *within* the American democratic system.

Pound remained disgusted by what his country had become, and continued to seek solace in the past. His essay, 'The Jefferson-Adams Letters as a Shrine and a Monument' is symptomatic of this.[8] The correspondence falls into two phases. The first volume relates to the late eighteenth century when the two were associates and rivals. The second volume relates to a resumed relationship in the last phase of their lives when in 1812 they patched up their differences and began a fourteen-year correspondence. It is this phase that produces some of the most delightful and learned writing between the two elderly Founding Fathers. It lasts practically till the day they both died – 4 July 1826. For Pound the correspondence serves two purposes. It allows him to dwell on his pessimism about American culture, lamenting his country's ignorance of its own history. He also finds that Jefferson's views on debt and banking are along similar lines to his own.

'Shrine' was published in the *North American Review*, Winter 1937–1938 issue. Pound starts by dividing American history into four phases. The first phase, 1780 to 1830, is that of 'American civilization'. The next phase, 1830 to 1860, is 'The period of thinning, of mental impoverishment, scission between life of the mind and life of the nation'. The third phase, 1870 to 1930, is 'The period of despair, civil war as hiatus . . . The division between the temper, thickness, richness of the mental life of Henry Adams, and Henry James, and that of say U. S. Grant, McKinley, Harding, Coolidge, and Hoover.' The last phase is, of course, the 1930s.

---

8 *The Adams-Jefferson Letters: The Complete Correspondence Between Thomas Jefferson and Abigail and John Adams*, in two volumes, edited by Lester J. Cappon, is the most recently available edition, and the one to which I refer. It is not clear from Pound's essay which edition he is using.

> The possibilities of revival, starting perhaps with a valorization of our cultural heritage, not merely as something lost in dim retrospect, a tombstone, tastily carved, whereon to shed dry tears or upon which to lay a few withered violets, in the manner of, let us say, the late Henry (aforementioned) Adams. The query being: should we lose or go on losing our own revolution (of 1776–1830) by whoring after exotics, Muscovite or European? ('Shrine', *SP*, p. 147)

Pound has a beef about American teaching of history, which he laments is sadly negligent of its glorious past. The *Letters* are great literature as well as history. 'Our national culture can be perhaps better defined from the Jefferson letters than from any other three sources, and mainly to its benefice' (*SP*, pp. 148–9).

Much is said thereafter about *paideuma* and the Mediterranean pre-Renaissance civilization, which I have quoted earlier in this book. But Pound's interest is in Jefferson – partly because he sees him as a stick with which to beat the later generation of American leaders; mainly because he deemed Jefferson a man whose attitude to money and debt he could approve of. As to the former Pound says, 'Jefferson's America was civilized while because its chief men were social. It is only in our gormy and squalid day that the chief American powers have been, and are, anti-social.'

Today we are much more aware of Jefferson's double standards as a champion of liberty who was also, and at the same time, a slave owner. But Pound's generation was much less critical.

The main issue for Pound is, however, debt and taxes. Jefferson had lived through the Revolution, which was financed pretty much from promissory notes issued by the rebels, to be redeemed against future revenues. The financing of the American War of Independence was, like many such liberation struggles, an experiment in innovative financing. The individual states were jealous of their powers and reluctant to grant what the troops wanted. Thus the Continental Congress requested $8 million and got from the states only $400,000. As the statesman Alexander Hamilton said, 'Power without revenue ... is a name.'[9] The states would not give Congress the power to collect taxes without a unanimous vote since it required a change in the Articles of Confederation. In the meantime the Army of the United States had to issue IOUs to feed itself.

It was realists like Hamilton who sought a new Constitutional framework which would give the US Congress tax-collecting powers, and it was the effort to do so that brought together the convention in Philadelphia which abandoned the old Constitution and adopted that which is still in force today. It was denounced at the time as a centralizing act but it was necessary in order to make the USA a viable military power. As we saw above, Hamilton had to persuade Congress to take over the debts incurred by the States as well as all the debts of the Union forces – IOUs that were circulating at a discount of nearly 75 per cent of their face value. Hamilton took the bold and very unpopular step of accepting all debt at par value. This was the least a 'newly emerging' or 'developing' country could do. It had to convince the Europeans, who had the capital to export, that the US had a fiscally responsible government. Unlike many of his detractors, Hamilton knew that if a state paid its debt charges promptly and fully it would be able to borrow more. Debt was a strength not a weakness. That was the lesson learnt from the revolutionary financial policies in Britain of Sir Robert Walpole, First Lord of the Treasury and thought of as the nation's first Prime Minister, which had checked French power in Europe in a hundred years of war. To this day, Britain's Prime Minister is also called the First Lord of the Treasury.

At the end of Hamilton's tenure as Secretary of the Treasury in 1795, when he told George Washington he wanted to retire, 'American finances were in good order ... the United States had the high-

[9] In what follows I have relied among other sources on Brookhiser, Richard, *Alexander Hamilton, American* (1999).

est credit rating in Europe of any nation, some of its bonds selling at 10 percent over par' (Brookhiser, p. 121). Only nowadays, with emerging markets and Third World economies struggling to establish such a credit rating, do we realize what a monumental effort this must have been for the then emerging USA. But this was lost on Hamilton's detractors. Jefferson was against Hamilton on many grounds, especially because he thought Hamilton pro-British. Also as a Virginia squire and slave owner, he was jealous of states' rights. Hamilton's proposals were giving the Union power against the individual states. It was only after he became President and faced the threat of war at sea and on land that Jefferson became aware of the need for sound finance. But he continued to oppose permanent debt along British lines because of his distrust of Federal power. Thus he wanted debt that would be retired in finite time. However, as remarked earlier, he happily arranged to borrow from European finance houses, including, indeed, Rothschild, to buy Louisiana from the French. Pound says nothing of this deft manoeuvre. He prefers his Jefferson as the sage, out of power, pronouncing on the state of the Union from the high ground of Monticello.

He quotes with approval Jefferson's dictum in his letter to William H. Crawford in 1816:

> [A]nd if the national bills issued be bottomed (as is indispensable) on pledges of specific taxes for their redemption within certain and moderate epochs, and be of proper denomination for circulation, no interest on them would be necessary or just, because they would answer to every one of the purposes of the metallic money and withdrawn and replaced by them.
> ('Shrine', *SP*, p. 152)

Jefferson is advocating the state issuing interest-free debt which it would redeem from hypothecated taxes. The debt has to be issued in small enough denominations to be circulable as notes for daily transactions. In those days, bills would circulate if they carried a good name on them – i.e. if the borrower's credit was sound. A moment's thought shows that in today's world that is just currency which the state can issue and it does not need to be redeemed. Gold Standard and other restrictions on money supply made this connection obscure but currency is interest-free debt issued by governments. The hypothecation of specific taxes makes the debt issuing more 'responsible' but also risky since one can never guarantee the yield of specific taxes. Today we do not hypothecate taxes but pool them in general revenue out of which government expenditure including debt servicing charges are met. The issue is not how the debt is issued but the prudence in issuing it so that it will benefit and not ruin the economy.

For Ezra Pound the important thing is that the state should not have to pay interest when it borrows. Its credit should be enough of a 'public good' for the private economy to grant it zero-interest debt. This is why he says of the Jefferson lines he quotes that they 'are eight of the most significant lines ever written'.

But typically states do not have such credit: it has to be earned. If the USA had issued such zero-interest debt, its notes would have circulated at a discount. That discount would be just another form of interest and Pound does not see that. Jefferson had within his lifetime seen state debt circulate at a discount and knew how difficult it would be to issue debt which would float at par value. That would require a reputation for fiscal responsibility. It cannot be asserted as a part of sovereignty even in a democratically elected regime.

Many people who make a fetish of interest payments and usury do not often see that if interest is not paid up front, there are many devices to extract it. Thus in many Islamic banking regimes, formal interest is neither charged nor earned but discounts and bonuses are frequently paid as camouflage for interest. If I borrow £1000 for one year I may either choose to pay 10 per cent interest or pay zero but get only £910 of my debt up front with £90 or roughly 10 per cent deducted at the start. Yet I repay the full £1000. So there is no usury, no *riba* but the economist will say there is still interest payment. For all his pursuit of economics, Pound thinks like a moralist not an economist.

For Pound, of course, Jefferson is contra-usury and so is the key to many things. He blamed the First World War on interest-bearing debt issued by European governments. Let me quote again:

> ... Europe went blind into that war because mankind had not digested Jefferson's knowledge. They went into that war because the canon law had been buried, because all general knowledge had been split up into useless or incompetent fragments. Because literature no longer bothered about the language of 'law and of the state' because the state and plutocracy cared less than a damn about letters. ('Shrine', *SP*, p. 153)

Of course during the Second World War, the USA gave money free of interest to Great Britain under Lend Lease while it had lent during the First World War. The only war debt Great Britain incurred was what it owed to the members of the British Empire, which took the form of sterling balances at the Bank of England. So usury did not impinge between the partners in the Atlantic Alliance and yet Great Britain could not borrow interest-free from its Imperial subjects. Thus usury can come and go!

Pound's argument needs to be challenged. Even if one were to grant a faint and indirect connection between the war and canon law and usury, it is hard to swallow the rest of it. Where is the evidence that literature (in what language?) no longer bothered about the language of law and the state? Coming as Pound's article does at the cusp of 1937 and 1938, what we see is a further descent into self-delusion on his part. He is now the sole Saviour of American civilization because he alone sees the truth of Jefferson. He deplores the lack of Latin in his contemporary world. He, of course, knew Latin as did Jefferson. This despair is then generalized into an apocalyptic vision of the world with a *tour d'horizon* involving Aquinas, Pierre Bayle, Rabelais, Flaubert, et al.

As Pound himself confesses,

> There may be a defect in the 'decline and fall' method in writing history. There is certainly a defect in it if the analyst persists in assuming that this or that institution (say the Church) 'fell' merely because some other paideuma or activity (organized formally, or sporadic and informal) arises, overcrowds, overshadows it, or merely gets greater publicity. ('Shrine', *SP*, p. 155)

Yet that is exactly how he takes the role of the relaxation of the ban on usury to be.

The next logical item in this series is 'National Culture: A Manifesto' (1938), which was first published in 1960 in *Impact: Essays on Ignorance and the Decline of American Civilization* (edited by Noel Stock). It is however of a piece with 'Shrine'. It starts with an autobiographical hint when Pound writes:

> A national American culture existed from 1770 till at least 1861. Jefferson could not imagine an American going voluntarily to inhabit Europe. After the debacle of American culture individuals had to emigrate in order to conserve such fragments of American culture as had survived. It was perhaps no less American but it was in a distinct sense less *nationally* American as the usurocracy came into steadily more filthy and damnable control of the Union. ('National Culture', *SP*, p. 161)

So by 1938 Pound had convinced himself that he had exiled himself because of the decline of American culture, and that the usurocracy was to blame for this decline. It is not unknown, presumptuous as it is, among diasporic intellectuals to think that they alone carry the true essence of their native land. In Pound's case it is of interest as a guide to his descent into the delusion that made him give those radio talks.

There is also a hint of self-pity as after acknowledging that William Carlos Williams is 'Whitman's living descendant' and 'is indelibly New England', Pound adds, 'There is I think little doubt that I should have more quickly attained a unity of expression had I been also New England without disorderly trek of four or five generations across the whole teeming continent' ('National Culture', *SP*, p. 164).

Could it be that the long-remembered taunts of the snobbish Westons against the footloose Pounds were now beginning to hurt, or was it merely a realization that he was not a top-drawer American literary figure?

But economics cannot wait much longer. 'I mean to say there is one point in the constitution which has not been tried and which the infamies infesting the White House for the past decades do not and dare not try: namely the right of Congress to determine the value of money' ('National Culture', *SP*, p. 165).

This last is a reference which recurs in Pound's later pamphlets to Article 1 section 8 of the American Constitution which states, *inter alia*,

> The Congress shall have power
> To coin Money, regulate the Value thereof, and of foreign Coin, and fix the Standard of Weights and Measures

Pound laments that Congress has given up on this obligation. But since the US Congress had just overhauled the Federal Reserve and regulated the banking system in an unprecedented set of laws such as the 1933 Glass-Steagall Act, it is difficult to believe that Pound would have been satisfied with anything less than being given charge of the currency himself. But how Congress could regulate the value of domestic coin except by urging prudent fiscal behaviour on the part of the Executive and regulating the Federal Reserve System (which it did) is also hard to fathom. Pound had a grudge against Roosevelt and other US

Presidents and he was not going to let facts stand in his way.[10]

By 1939, Pound was beginning desperately to want to do something to keep his country out of the impending war. He went back for a visit, which was a failure from that point of view. His disquiet about American cultural and political decline (as he thought of it) was not allayed. From here on, there is a shriller note in the pamphlets, and by the time war breaks out things are out of hand. The anti-Semitism that he is to express vociferously in his radio broadcasts and elsewhere begins to creep in now. However, much of his economics and even his cultural despair do not stem from his anti-Semitism, but from his sense of increasing alienation from America while all the time convinced that, if he is not the only one, he is one of the very few who understand the true nature of American civilization – a civilization he believes to be in danger of being lost through the philistinism of the usurocracy. He convinces himself in Rapallo that he alone can save the American Constitution.

The pamphlet 'What Is Money For?' came out in 1939 and was reissued in 1951. It is catechistic, being divided into small sections with definitions. It begins by stating that money is a measure of price, a means of exchange and a guarantee of future exchange or, as we would put it now, a store of value. The aim of money for Pound 'is to fix things so that decent people can eat, have clothes and houses up to the limit of available goods'.

The value of money has to be established in terms of work or some real product. 'Sovereignty inheres in the right to ISSUE money (tickets) and to determine the value thereof.' The logical conclusion of this right and what the American Constitution Article 1/8 says about the power of the Congress implied that 'Hence

---

10 There has been a strong political interest in making the Money interest subservient to Public interest in the USA through much of the twentieth century to which Pound seldom alludes. See Mehrling, Perry, *Money Interest and Public Interest: American Monetary Thought 1920-1970* (1997).

the US Government could establish the JUST PRICE, and a just price system.'

This is because: 'Only the STATE can effectively fix the JUST PRICE of any commodity by means of state-controlled pools of raw products and the restoration of guild organization in industry' ('Money', *SP*, pp. 290–3, *passim*).

The desirable quantity of money then is that which would provide full employment. 'It is the business of the STATE to see that there is enough money in the hands of the WHOLE people, and in adequately rapid EXCHANGE, to effect distribution of all wealth produced and produceable' ('Money', *SP*, p. 293). This was proposed by Douglas but was not carried out in England and the USA. But 'Mussolini and Hitler wasted very little time PROPOSING. They started and DO distribute BOTH tickets and actual goods on various graduated scales according to the virtues and activities of Italians and Germans' ('Money', *SP*, p. 293).

This contrast of Germany and Italy with the USA and the UK was not out of step with what was happening. Whatever their later atrocities, in the thirties the fascist states did manage full employment through planning and restrictions that the liberal economies did not implement. Pound adds that Douglas was not happy about the lack of democracy in those countries which had followed his advice:

> BUT for the monetary scientist or economist the result is the same. The goods are being distributed ... Ten or more years ago I said that Mussolini had achieved more than Douglas, because Douglas has presented his ideas as a greed system, not as a will system. ('Money', *SP*, p. 294).

Either way, he feels, this system is preferable to the dole, which degrades British workers.

The rest of the pamphlet covers familiar ground – inflation, Gesell, Jefferson's statement on zero-interest debt circulating as money, the distinction between property and capital, etc. There is then a section on usury, where Lenin and Hitler are cited as saying similar things about the power of finance and capital on an international scale. This he follows up with a series of statements about Jews.

> I wish to distinguish between prejudice against the Jew as such and the suggestion that the Jew should face his own problem.
> Does he in his individual case wish to observe the law of Moses? . . .
> Does he propose to continue to rob other men by usury mechanism while wishing to be considered a 'neighbour'? . . .
> This is the sort of double-standard which a befouled English delegation tried to enforce via the corrupt League of Nations (frontage and face wash for the worst international corruption at Basel) . . .
> USURY is the cancer of the world, which only the surgeon's knife of Fascism can cut out of the life of nations.
> ('Money', *SP*, pp. 299–300)

William Cookson, the editor of *Selected Prose*, from which this has been taken, offers a footnote at this stage trying to show that Pound was not anti-Semitic by citing other statements. Pound said various things on either side of the anti-Semitic divide. But as I said at the outset, it is not worth contesting that Pound was at times, and increasingly so in the period 1939–45, anti-Semitic and fascist. What is remarkable about the sentences quoted above is that they conclude the pamphlet. There are appendices and quotes but the pamphlet finishes on that note about fascism cutting out the cancer of usury with which it associates the Jews.

However, as I commented earlier, Pound's economics are separable from his prejudices even though he did not separate them. His contemporary relevance is as a thinker about money and work and distribution and full employment. His obsessions about usury can be divorced from his increasing hatred of Jews during the War.

V
War and the Descent into Despair

The character of Pound's writing over the next few years is repetitive and more pessimistic. Money and American culture remain his primary themes, and little that is new is added except that it is all more shrill, more self-centred, more apocalyptic. He also now writes in Italian as well as in English. The Italian pamphlets were translated in English after the War. *A Visiting Card* was published in Italian in 1942, and in English by Peter Russell in 1952. *Gold and Work* (*GW*) was written in Italian in 1944 and translated and published in 1951. 'An Introduction to the Economic Nature of the United States' was written in 1944 and translated and published in 1950. The very fact that Pound had begun writing in Italian shows another layer of his perceived rejection and self-exile. Now he was in triple exile – from the USA, from England and France, and finally from the English language as his preferred mode of communication. The two Cantos, LXXII and LXXIII, are also in Italian. It is only after his capture that he returns to English in his *Pisan Cantos*. (Though some of the *Pisan Cantos* seem to have been written earlier than in 1945, see below for a quote from LXXVIII). He continued to correspond in English, but nevertheless his adoption of the Italian language was a declaration of some significance. Perhaps he did genuinely expect Mussolini to win the war and hoped thereby to vindicate his exile.

VC is bitty, as is the case of all the pamphlets after *ABC* – presented in small sections rather than a long argument. But Pound starts with a stark statement about the end of liberty, quoting a radio broadcast from Berlin asserting the absolute power of the State. So what of liberty, his constant concern, until now? '. . . [W]ith the decadence of the democratic – or republican – state this definition [of liberty as the right to do anything that does not injure others] has been betrayed in the interests of usurers and speculators.' The root of this is an error in understanding the nature of money. Marx and John Stuart Mill got it wrong.

> Money does not contain energy. The half-lira piece cannot *create* the platform ticket, the cigarettes, or piece of chocolate that issues from the slot-machine... But it is by this piece of legerdemain that humanity has been thoroughly trussed up, and it has not yet got free. (*VC, SP*, pp. 307–8)

The connection between usury and the war is now direct and simple. It is transparent to the monetary scientist that Pound has called himself. Old obsessions recur:

> The war in which brave men are being killed and wounded, our own war here and now, began – or rather the phase we are now fighting began – in 1694, with the foundation of the Bank of England...
>
> Said Paterson in his manifesto addressed to prospective shareholders, 'the bank hath benefit of the interest on all moneys which it creates out of nothing'...
>
> This swindle, calculated to yield interest at the usurious rate of sixty per cent was impartial. It hit friends and enemies alike. (*VC, SP*, p. 308)

As I have mentioned before, it is not clear where the quote from Paterson comes. Christopher Hollis, whose book *The Two Nations* Pound cites, does not give the source. It is not in the document known as *A Brief Account of the intended Bank of England*, whose authorship is attributed to William Paterson or Michael Godfrey (the first Deputy Governor of the Bank). But even if it was said in a prospectus by Paterson, it is factually and analytically untrue. Banks do not create credit out of nothing. For one thing the directors of the original Bank had to subscribe the £1.2 million (Paterson subscribed £2,400 when he became Director but resigned after one year following a dispute) and ever afterwards maintain the good credit of the Bank by balancing its assets against its liabilities. Interest rates far from being the sixty per cent which haunts Pound's imagination came down in England after the establishment of the Bank. After all, the Dutch already had such a bank and the English were just copying it for their own use. Indeed Paterson's proposal was criticized by Tory interests as importing something foreign to England. As Paterson himself remarked 'Others said this project came from Holland and therefore would not hear of it, since we had too many Dutch things already.'[1] Blaming the Second World War on the establishment in 1694 of the Bank of England is the final goodbye to any reasoned argument that Pound could have made in favour of his radical money proposals. It is a hyperbole gone mad as perhaps its author was going.

Writing in Italian, presumably for an Italian readership, Pound sinks further into gloom as he writes:

> Our culture lies shattered in fragments, and with the monetology of usurocracy our common culture has become a closed book to the aesthetes...
>
> Your revolution is our revolution; and ours was, and is, yours: against a common, putrescent enemy. The peasant feeds us and the gombeen-man strangles us – if he cannot suck our blood by degrees. (*VC, SP*, p. 309)

After this follows a summary sketch of American history but this time it starts with the founding of 'the stinking bank' – the Bank of England. Then the ban against Pennsylvania issuing its own

---

[1] The quotation is from a two-volume collection of Paterson's writings cited in Acres, W. Marston *The Bank of England From Within 1694–1900*, Vol I, p. 7 (1931). Acres gives as his source Paterson Vol 2, pp. 67–8. I have checked these two volumes as well for the quote given by Pound without success.

money in 1750 and in 1776 the American Revolution.[2] A small matter of taxation (without representation) is ignored in this version under the rubric: 'A number of different, secondary events are mentioned in the obscurantist text-books administered to the victims in the schools and universities of the USA.' Pound has thus adopted the totalitarian propaganda style of writing off the American citizenry as victims.

Then, after mentioning Hamilton pejoratively, Pound extols 1830–40 for 'The war of the people against the Bank [of the United States], won by the people under the leadership of Jackson and Van Buren.'

The Civil War is described as between debtors and creditors 'on the moral pretext that the debtors possessed negro slaves'.

This is another rewrite of what Pound had earlier said of the Civil War as one in which a million had died for 'negro freedom'. But more important for Pound is the next statement: 'Right in the middle of this war the Government was betrayed and the people were sold into the hands of the Rothschilds, through the intermediaries John Sherman, Ikleheimer and Van der Gould.'

This story of a conspiracy to enslave the USA to the Rothschilds is a new element in Pound's history of the USA. He quotes from Willis A. Overholser's *The History of Money in the United States* to the effect that the European capitalists would use the debt incurred in the Civil War to control the money supply. What is

---

2 Pound is confused about the Pennsylvania case. The relevant authority was not the Bank of England but the Board of Trade and the currency was not banned in 1750. Pennsylvania was issuing paper currency against loans from 1723 till the mid-1760s. English merchants welcomed it since Pennsylvania was able to export its gold and silver for foreign trade while using paper currency at home. It was the Board of Trade which got worried about this export of gold on mercantilist grounds, and in 1764, the British Parliament passed an Act prohibiting any American colony from issuing paper money as legal tender. Lester, Richard A., *Monetary Experiments: Early American and Recent Scandinavian* (1939) contains the details, pp. 56–111.

probably more to the point is that America needed European capital at this stage in her history to absorb immigrant labour and build the manufacturing and transport structures. This was one of the most rapid growth periods of her history, which at the end of it, in 1914, saw America emerge as a world power with an income exceeding that of Great Britain and France together. The history of the inflation due to greenbacks and the effort to retire them from 1875 onwards is well-known.[3] The point, however, is that America prospered in the fifty years after the end of the Civil War rather than stagnated. There was a decline in agricultural prices but this was part of a worldwide trend and not a solely American phenomenon. But Pound was young at the time of William Jennings Bryan and the struggle against gold and thus accepts the anti-banking version of US history.

Since this pamphlet is for an Italian readership, Pound mentions quite a few Italian as well as other European authors as they relate to his view of money – Demosthenes to Dante, Salmasius to Butchart, and so on. The basic point remains the same as always:

> Credit is a social product. It does not depend on the individual alone. The confidence you have that I will pay you 100 lire in ten years' time depends on the social order, the degree of civilization, the probabilities and possibilities of the human congeries . . .
>
> To say that the state cannot take action or create something because it 'lacks the money' is as ridiculous as saying that it 'can't build roads because it's got no kilometres'. (*VC, SP*, p. 311)

He finds much in Mazzini to agree with and volunteers this:

> I insist on the identity of our American Revolution of 1776 with your Fascist Revolution. Two chapters in the same war against the usurers, the same who crushed Napoleon.

[3] Friedman, M. and A. Schwartz *A Monetary History of the United States 1867–1960* (1963), Chapters 2 to 4.

THE ROUTE OF ALL EVIL

Writing this in the middle of a war in which America regarded Italy as an enemy country cannot have helped him later. But it is the sort of daft generous thing people say when they are sheltering with an enemy of their country. So did Lord Haw-Haw and even P. G. Wodehouse. Pound then quotes Robert Mond (brother of Alfred Mond who was head of ICI) from his Canto LXXVIII to the effect that having crushed Napoleon it will not take twenty years to crush Mussolini once the sanctions (after the Abyssinia War) had been imposed. He adds: 'Fortunately these messes have no sense of proportion, or the world would already be under their racial domination.'

The quote is given backwards in the pamphlet but it goes:

> 'and the economic war has begun'
>   Napoleon wath a goodth man, it took uth
>   20 yearth to cruwth him
> it will not take uth 20 years to cruwth Mussolini . . .

Though this Canto is part of the *Pisan Cantos*, it was written not in the Pisa jail but before that. The lisp is obviously meant to be a sign of Mond's Jewishness. As it happens, Mond was wrong only in overestimating how long it took to crush Mussolini.

VC ranges over more than just money matters. All the old familiars are there – Gesell, Wörgl, and so on – but Pound wanders into history and literature (at one stage comparing himself with Eliot), quoting E. E. Cummings's 'Dirge', and then comes back to Social Credit and Jefferson. There is a large amount of Chinese material here but on the whole it rambles on to include many of the things Pound had on his mind. The picture is of a lonely man who has no one to talk to so pours it all out into a pamphlet.

The pamphlet shows Pound now committed to the Fascist cause. He has broken the umbilical cord, and while still regarding himself as an American, he has taken Fascism as his credo. He thinks he is still only propagating social credit, but the tone has changed. Usury and its ills now weigh much more heavily than the old concern about full employment and distribution. There will be no going back.

GW, written in 1944, when Mussolini was already in the Republic of Salo, is written in an elegiac vein. It starts with a description of a utopia in which all children get a decent education. But soon Pound gets down to all the old themes. There are the recurrent passages on the Bank of England, Jefferson, the American Civil War and how the USA was sold to the Rothschilds, etc. Parallel to this is 'An Introduction to the Economic Nature of the United States'. Here again there is a financial history of the USA repeating some of the earlier stuff.

We start with the colonizers trying to use paper money and the Bank of England stopping them. Pound praises Adams as he raises debt in Europe for the fledgling Union. Raising foreign money was essential for them; even Jefferson as Ambassador to Paris was engaged in the same enterprise. Pound does not seem to mind this as much as raising money abroad later after the Civil War. But Hamilton is criticized for assuming the debt of the Union and the states although he was only trying to establish the credit of the new Republic.

Pound takes his readers through an account of financial developments – railroad scandals, the trial of J. P. Morgan – and excoriates the speculators and brokers. There is a rambling story of the grandfather Pound and his wife who was the daughter of a New York Justice of the Peace who lost $100,000 in a bank failure. And, as always, the gloom about America and usury.

> Usury ruined the Republic. Usury has been defined as too high an interest on money. The word finance became fashionable in the bankpaper era. And it is to this that Jefferson alludes in the phrase: 'No one has a natural right to be money-lender save him who has it to lend.' With the 'financial' era, the word usury disappeared from polite conversation.
> ('Economic Nature', *SP* p. 174)

It is difficult to imagine today that Pound was writing about what even in the 1930s was the most prosperous country in the world. On the other hand, he might surprise a modern reader by coming out as someone who cares about conservation:

> The 'Economic' history of the United States is, in a sense, the history of enormous waste of the immense natural resources, waste that took place because no immediate need for conservation was apparent and, in many instances, did not exist.
> ('Economic Nature', *SP*, p. 175)

Further on the theme recurs:

> The American tragedy is a continuous history of waste – waste of the natural abundance first, then waste of the new abundance offered by the machine, and then by machines, no longer isolated, but correlated and centuplicating the creative power of human labour . . .
> The improvident Americans killed bison without thought of protecting them. Forests were cut down without thought of conservation. This had no immediate effect on the prosperity of the inhabitants, because of nature's abundance.
> ('Economic Nature', *SP* p. 176)

But of course the enemy is not far behind.

> The usurers, now called financiers, plotted against abundance . . . Polite society did not consider usury as Dante did, that is, damned to the same circle of Hell as the sodomites, both acting against the potential abundance of nature.
> ('Economic Nature', *SP*, p. 176)

There follows once again a financial history with Van Buren extolled for having fought against the Bank of the United States. The quotes from Van Buren's memoirs make no sense unless one goes into the history of the fight against the Bank that Van Buren waged. Pound takes it for granted that everyone knows it or will take his word for it. More of the history is given but now the emphasis is on the disgraceful surrender to the usurious interests. There are two chronological outlines with a lot of overlap and more of the history told episodically. It is as if Pound is in a hurry to tell everything at once in case time runs out – as indeed it was now running out.

'America, Roosevelt and the Causes of the Present War' is also written in Italian. It was published in Venice in 1944 and reprinted in 1951 in an English translation. Much of 'America' is already contained in 'Economic Nature' and many other publications. By now, Pound is rewriting the same essay as often as he can. It was obviously put out as war propaganda by the Italians. Pound was the biggest catch for the Fascists, and he was a willing recruit to their cause. At the outset of 'America', the message is clear:

> This war was not caused by any caprice on Mussolini's part, nor on Hitler's. This war is part of the secular war between usurers and peasants, between usurocracy and whomever does an honest day's work with his own brain or hands.
> ('America', p. 5)

Once more we get the autobiographical story about the grandfather already recounted in *VC*. There we are told how he started a railway with only $5000 cash and how he printed his own money. He only found this out when his father Homer brought some old newspaper clipping to Rapallo. In 'America', he adds, 'In 1878 my grandfather said the same things that I'm saying now but the memory of his efforts has been obliterated.'

Further on in the pamphlet, we are given a hint as to what it was that grandfather Pound had said: 'In 1878 a member got up in Congress and expressed the hope that he might keep some of the non-interest bearing National debt in circulation as currency' ('America', p. 13).

Since much of 'America' is repetition, only the occasional new item need be noted. By now of course Italy had dual government in Rome and then the Republic of Salo in the north where Mussolini was holed up. Pound was with Mussolini. So he repeats the parallel between the young American Republic and the Italian Republic of the day and warns about betrayal. Hamilton has now an added Jewish origin foisted upon him.

'Hamilton's racial origins have never been determined with certainty, though his eloquence, suavity, and drawing-room talents suggest a certain affinity with the abilities of Disraeli' ('America', p. 9). Hamilton was illegitimate at birth, being the child of Rachel Fawcett Lavine and a Scottish merchant James Hamilton on the Caribbean island of Nevis, and this was known to many of his contemporaries but he rose due to his abilities as a soldier, a legislator, a lawyer and finally as a finance minister. There has been no evidence that he was a Jew.

Pound has become convinced that Lincoln's assassination was a conspiracy on the part of the usurers. His favourite quotation from Lincoln (see Chapter 3 of his 'Introductory Textbook', *SP*, pp. 159–60) was from a letter the President wrote to Colonel E. Taylor about the origin of the greenbacks, the currency issued in the Civil War which financed the North's war effort. Pound quotes Lincoln as saying, '. . . and gave the people of this Republic the greatest blessing they ever had – their own paper to pay their own debt.' Pound then adds, 'Lincoln was assassinated after he made the statement given above.' As the statement was in a private letter and could not have been generally known in Lincoln's lifetime, it is not clear how it incited an assassination conspiracy. But that is a minor detail and Pound continues:

> The theatrical gesture of the assassin does not explain how it happened that he escaped from Washington after the alarm had been raised, by the *only* road that was not guarded; nor its synchronization with the attempted assassination of Seward,

the Secretary of State, nor various details of the affair. The fact remains that Lincoln had assumed a position in clear opposition to the usurocracy. ('America', p. 11)

For the conspiracy-minded it is all absolutely clear. Everything and anything that occurs can be traced back to the centre of the conspiracy – in Pound's case usurocracy. It spans centuries and even without a central office can still wreak havoc. Yet it has its headquarters:

> The usurers' assault was launched from London and Washington, united in operation. In 1863 the central office was in London, the branch in New York. To-day the position is reversed: the headquarters across the Atlantic, and the branch in London. The role of France is known. Mussolini was condemned by the international usurocracy from the moment he discovered the connexion between the usurers in New York and their creatures in Moscow. This is all very well known throughout Italy. ('America', p. 15)

'America' ends with the following words:

> The reason for the present publication, at this particular moment [a footnote explains in the Fascist Republican (i.e. Salo) Italy 1944] is to indicate the incidence of the present war in the series of wars provoked by the same never-dying agency, namely the world *usurocracy*, or the congregation of High Finance: Roosevelt, being in all this a kind of malignant tumour, not autonomous, not self-created, but an unclean exponent of something less circumscribed than his own evil personal existence; a magistrate with *legally* limited jurisdiction, a perjurer, not fully aware of what he does, why he does it, or where it leads to. His political life ought to be brought *sub judice*. ('America', p. 18)

These were the last words Pound published in prose, at least before he was arrested and sent for trial to Washington. It was his life not Roosevelt's which was brought *sub judice*. He had burnt his boats by then. His pessimism about American culture had turned into a paranoid historical vision of how America had become a victim of the usurocracy. This transformation is very rapid after the start of the war. What in 'Shrine' he expresses mild irritation about – the ignorance Americans have of their own history, or how the likes of Jefferson are not in contemporary politics – becomes a vicious and never-ending conspiracy that started before 1776. Everything is coloured by this – from the false glorification of the Boston Tea Party rather than Pennsylvania's experiment with paper currency as a crucial episode leading to the Declaration of Independence, the machinations of the (to Pound) possibly Jewish Hamilton to capture the USA in usurocracy by starting a bank, the way (in his view) Jackson and Van Buren have been ignored in American universities, the origin of the Civil War in usurocracy's hatred of slavery since it prevented cheap labour, the assassination of Lincoln because he championed greenbacks, the purchase of the USA by the Rothschilds, etc., etc. It is a genius brain going berserk and falling for its own fabrications and delusions. It is all laced with seeming erudition with a quotation from here and from there (and since these are obscure quotes, their very obscurity is proof of their suppression by the conspiracy) being harnessed into indicating a vast conspiracy of shady, unseen but powerful forces. (And if those in the conspiracy have names, they are, by chance, Jewish names.)

There is no regret or remorse on Pound's part that he wrote as he did. The fact that he encouraged the publications of these pamphlets in the 1950s while he was in St Elizabeth's, shows that he never disowned his views or actions; neither did he even see the necessity to write a new introduction explaining why he did what he did. His later association with shady characters, like John

Kasper, with White Supremacist sympathies, and his resumption of his fascist association after his return to Italy in 1958 tell us that the genius was not all innocent.

If he plunged steadily into a kind of madness starting from perfectly sane beginnings in 1933, Pound never tried to get back to level ground after the war had been fought and Fascism had lost. His good sense on monetary reform while not fully analytically worked out (as Keynes had done) was still informed by a deep humanism in as much as he hated men and women being economically deprived. He wanted full employment, shorter working hours, cheaper money, with the state being able to take over the money supply and perhaps even provide a national dividend. Much of this was achieved, albeit in a milder form, in the 1950s across developed capitalist countries. There was national control over money supply, gold became irrelevant in domestic affairs, the Bank of England was nationalized, a Welfare State had been established with some minimum social security.

But by then he had lost interest in the contemporary world. He was disengaged and the passion he brought to economic issues in the interwar period never recurred. He became a poet and a literary mentor again and a sage of a kind, a flawed patriarch who had brought disgrace to the Family but was still the best thing that the Family had to show off. His enormities had to be forgiven because not doing so would have required that he be punished for them and the punishment could only have been death.

VI
Pound Foolish?

Ezra Pound remains a puzzle after all these years. A pioneer of Modernism in poetry; a harbinger of the Future with Wyndham Lewis in their Vorticist phase; a generous helper of other geniuses; a man of stunningly cosmopolitan tastes in literature, ranging over all Western and some Eastern languages; a serious student of monetary schemes of writers such as Douglas and Gesell, and indeed a thinker of these issues in his own right. A polymath in his reading and his works, he still managed to become a partisan of an anti-Modern movement such as fascism, and became infected with a virulent anti-Semitism which is about as against cosmopolitanism as one can go. He became enamoured of a conspiracy theory about usurocracy and gave it credence when a short reflection, or talking to his old friends in London, would have cured him of such silliness. He betrayed his country of origin in the middle of a war in the mistaken belief that he alone had seen the truth about America, and thus permanently harmed his reputation so that it is very difficult to speak of his writings as one can of the likes of Joyce, Hemingway, Yeats or Eliot.

I have examined in some detail all Pound's prose writings on economic and monetary issues. It is possible, indeed essential to separate his positive and constructive thinking about economic matters from his vicious and negative conspiratorial writings. One way to do this, as I have attempted, is to look chronologically at his writings. There are three themes mixed up in all his prose writings. Principal is his concern with the life of the artists in America and the economic difficulties experienced by artists. This grows into an exploration of the roots of this weakness and the realization that perhaps America was not always a fringe of European culture happy with the crumbs that fell from the tables of London and Paris. The discovery of the Jefferson-Adams correspondence is one aspect of this. The story of why American culture slipped from its robust beginnings in the eighteenth century to its late-nineteenth-century debility is one ingredient in the eventual witches' brew that Pound made for his own destruction. He did not take the view that the debility was perhaps because America had cut itself off from the best of Europe after a few decades of independence. After all, Adams and Jefferson and Hamilton were members of a European culture; a reading of the Adams-Jefferson letters is enough to convince anyone of that. It seemed astonishing to Pound that two elder statesmen should be able to correspond in such fine style deploying a vast reading in several languages, not because it was a distinctively American phenomenon but because it was a perfectly natural thing for eighteenth-century Enlightenment European statesmen and politicians to do so. Adams and Jefferson are American pioneers but they are European intellectuals. It is only later, with Andrew Jackson – that is, after John Quincy Adams, who was the last of the older tradition – that America becomes increasingly inward-looking, and it re-entered the European world only after the Wilsonian intervention in the First World War.

Pound did not, indeed perhaps could not, take such a view because the milieu he belonged to on the East Coast had not severed its links with Europe. He had an education in all the European languages, classical and modern. He had been to Europe as a child and again as soon as he felt rejected by his own native land. But out there on the West Coast where he was born, Europe was a distant presence. Pound could see that East Coast literary culture was derivative and happy with hand-me-downs from London. The plight of the writer was hardly better in Europe at that time than in America, but even so Pound himself found more support in London than he did in New York when he returned in 1911. America was not yet ready for him. He was an exotic item in the salons of London but just a normal American in New York. Nevertheless, William Carlos Williams, E. E. Cummings, Hilda Doolittle, and others managed to make a living and write poetry in America. This is perhaps the reason for Pound's late regret in his 1938 piece 'National Culture' that William Carlos Williams was the genuine successor of Walt Whitman and his feeling that if only his family had taken root in New England, rather than wandered all over America, he could have attained 'a unity of expression'.

The route Pound took to understand American culture went quite by accident through the economic detour. His discovery of the economic/social issue dates from the First World War and especially after the death of Gaudier-Brzeska. It is then that he discovered Douglas and embraced his theory with a convert's zeal. Yet again he does not write about economics until 1933. His complaints about American culture and bureaucracy continue and he gets dyspeptic when he speaks of customs inspectors in New York. But these remain cranky laments, not as yet a worked-out story of why America has gone the way it has. There are hints, of course, as early as 1912 in *Patria Mia*. There were hordes in the streets of American cities who were a different sort from him and his family. If they had really loved their native soil, they would never have left. But then he had left; did he not love his native soil? Of course he did; even more than those who had stayed behind and he would show them by worrying constantly about the quality of culture 'back home'. Hence his never-flagging engagement with America – its culture, its politics, its economy. The farther he moves away from it – to London, to Paris to Rapallo – the deeper the sense of engagement gets. Whether it was also a recompense for his rejection by the fraternities in his university student days is difficult to say, but he was exiling himself farther and farther from America while writing about it constantly.

The economic writing is genuinely inspired by the misery around him and what he reads about his native land. At first he is concerned and quite creative in arguing the case for a Douglasite reform. *ABC* is a long pamphlet in which his economic philosophy is displayed and it is singularly free of prejudice or conspiracy theories about usury. He wants shorter working hours. He wants a monetary system that would take the responsibility of finding work for everyone and enough income (certificates) for people to be able to buy what they lack. The shortage of money is the main problem and while banks are the culprits they are not as yet run by sinister Jewish usurocrats. It is not that Douglas is absolutely right but like many pioneers he saw a problem clearly which orthodoxy could not see. Pound takes Douglas but brings ordinary American common sense to it because he is not interested in dogmatic disputes between Douglas and Gesell supporters or communists. He wants to explain as simply as he can why money should be just a means to provide full employment rather than be run on some orthodox principles.

This Pound has a lot to offer to the modern anti-globalizer or activist for development of poor countries. He raises fundamental questions about what the purpose of an economic system is – is it to serve the people, or to rule over them in pursuit of some abstract goal? Of course, economics has moved on and Keynes was able to convince the world of policy-makers that the economic system should see full employment as its goal. But again the monetarist backlash against Keynes has shifted the ground back to orthodoxy and there is an open argument especially in the case of developing countries whether the policies being urged on them by the IMF or the World Bank are not really pre-Keynesian economics in another guise. The entire issue of debt and its repayment is currently haunting many poor countries and despite much pious sentiment on the part of rich countries there is yet a need for public action to argue the case for debt forgiveness as the Jubilee 2000 campaign did.

So why, and indeed when, did this humanist modernist

reformer with a generous programme for redistribution and full employment become the dark partisan of a conspiracy theory steeped in anti-Semitism? When did he abandon modernism and take up obscurantism? Is the trigger something in the world out there or in something he read? Or was it something within him that turned him away from his previous self? It is possible in my view to draw a line somewhere around 1939 to separate the two Pounds. From 1933 till about 1939, he wrote essays and pamphlets (see Chapter IV) where he is a sane, reasonable person patiently arguing for his reform programme or discoursing on American culture and history. Once war starts, he switches to writing in Italian as we have seen in the four pamphlets covered in Chapter V and the tone gets distinctly vicious. What has happened?

For one thing, in the late 1930s he was getting involved more and more with Oswald Mosley's Blackshirts movement, writing for their journal *Fascist Quarterly* and in their newspaper *Action* (Stock, pp. 349–50). He was also writing in Seward Collins's *American Review*, and to Congressmen, academics and politicians in the US about Social Credit and monetary reform. Some, such as the economist Irving Fisher, replied to him and took interest in matters such as the Gesellian proposal of stamp scrip; Senator Borah, on the other hand, replied very tersely thrice to Pound's twenty-seven letters. Pound's advice to his countrymen became a mixture of condescension and abuse, hectoring and cajoling and his friends grew worried by his increasingly bitter tone and attitude. Thus William Carlos Williams wrote to him, 'I think that if anyone needs a change, a new viewpoint, it's you. You can't even smell the stink you're in any more' (Torrey, p. 151, quoting unpublished correspondence). Ford Madox Ford tried to get him a job in the USA but Olivet College in Michigan was too modest for Pound and from all accounts he spoiled his chances by bypassing Ford and trying to deal with the President of the College in a high-handed manner (Torrey, pp. 151–2).

It was, however, his trip to the US in 1939 that I think must have been the turning point. This was his first visit since 1911. He was now a famous poet and a well-known personality, and he expected to be taken seriously at the highest level for his policy ideas. The Italian government paid his fare, first-class, so much did they need his advocacy in Washington. He arranged to talk to the economists at Harvard and to politicians in Washington, and to lecture at Harvard. He was hoping that he might be asked to advise Roosevelt about Europe and economics. He was to be given a Honorary Doctorate by his old alma mater, Hamilton College, and he could have expected a triumphant return. But he was disappointed. They all listened to him politely but did not ask him to do anything more. Roosevelt had no time for him.

His sympathetic biographer Noel Stock writes of his trip:

> Pound was depressed because he was not having the success in Washington that he thought he might have, either with regard to monetary reform or in finding an advisory position through which he might place his knowledge of Europe, history and economics at the service of his country. The ideas he had for the building of a better America seemed to be falling on deaf ears or to be doomed to suffer transformation in the machinery of political compromise, machinery now thoroughly suspect owing to Roosevelt's disregard for the constitution. (Stock, p. 362)

Even the rather more hostile E. Fuller Torrey writes:

> He had talked with senators, lectured at Harvard, and received an honorary degree – things he had longed to do – yet his trip had not really been a success. As he boarded the Italian liner for his return, he must have wondered what he had to do to get the full attention of his countrymen. (Torrey, p. 154)

What he had to do was to show them that he could bite back. The

1939 visit was yet another rejection of the prodigal by America. He had been excluded from fraternities while at college, he did not make it to a doctoral degree at Pennsylvania, did not get the offers he wanted when he went back in 1911, had no serious offers of a job in the USA all these years, and now when he was willing and eager to offer his advice to keep America out of the European war, he was spurned. He would show them who really cared for America and her Constitution.

As he fashioned for himself this role of the true but rejected American, Pound began to reach into his roots and discovered the prejudices of the East Coast WASP. In *Patria Mia* he had already remarked on the influx from Europe. While at Harvard during his 1939 visit, he had noticed that there were many Jews at his lecture and so he deliberately played up his anti-Semitism; likewise, he refused when in New York to go into a bookshop because it was run by Frances Steloff, a Jew and indeed a fan of his. To quote Stock again:

> He had inherited the anti-Semitism of the East Coast American, directed against the coarseness and habits as well as the racial traits of Jewish immigrants; but this was possibly not much more than a faint sense of superiority, unpleasant perhaps but not necessarily dangerous.

Perhaps not, but a reading of *Patria Mia* would tell us otherwise. In any case this 'harmless' anti-Semitism of his young days, if that was what it was, could now flower into a full-scale venomous prejudice in the fascist climate of the late 1930s. He could dredge up all the stuff he may have read, or heard of, such as the Protocols of Zion, and proceed to believe and spout it (even though the Protocols document was proved to be a forgery in 1921, it continued to surface in anti-Semitic campaigns up to the end of the war).

But even if this fertile ground had not been prepared, Pound was treading the path of many who join utopian monomaniacal sects.

They start with lofty principles, a clear analysis and a single answer – a cure-all. If the world is not immediately convinced, they become abusive and seek answers for the perversity of this world that refuses to be saved. They soon find a conspiracy against them, hidden but well organized. Major Douglas went the same path as Pound. As John Finlay says in his study of Social Credit,

> In the beginning he was restrained in his attitude towards it. But from an early belief that it might, 'like Topsy, just have growed', he moved to attack 'a very deeply laid and well considered plot of enslaving the industrial world to the German-American – Jewish – financiers'. It was not long before the German-American element faded into the background, leaving the Jews as the real villains of the piece. When asked where real power lay, Douglas would answer that it was with Sir Basil Zaharoff, the mysterious armament king. (Finlay, p. 103).

Yet Finlay refuses to label this anti-Jewish attitude anti-Semitic. He is however honest enough to cite several passages from Douglas's speeches which leave little doubt as to where Douglas was heading.

> If I have, for my own part, come to believe that there is a fundamental relationship between the troubles which afflict Europe and what is known as the Jewish problem, I have formed that opinion with reluctance ... perhaps the first necessity is to explain beyond any risk of misunderstanding, the nature of the charge, and why it is a racial and not a personal indictment. In this connection, Disraeli's description of his people as 'a splendidly organized race' is significant. Organization has much of the tragedy of life to its debt; and organization is a Jewish speciality. (Finlay, p. 104)

There is no reason why the Social Credit doctrine should be anti-Semitic. As a theory, it is a pale and somewhat restrictive version of a theory of deficient effective demand. No conspiracy, whether by Jews or any other group, is necessary to explain why it might be an explanation of unemployment and why it might yet be inadequate as a cure. One can be against bankers and moneylenders and high interest rates and even usury without becoming anti-Semitic. Pound managed throughout the 1930s to do just that. It is only when the war began, and perhaps his sense of rejection got hold of his reasoning faculties, that he went off the edge. And once you go off the edge there is a lot of fake erudition you can display, delving into ancient and medieval history, philosophy and theology; even the occult can be brought in. Obscure and unread books become central to the propagation of the doctrine and the fact that others may not have heard of the books is proof positive that 'they' are preventing you from finding out the truth. Snippets of quotations free of context are given and events long forgotten are said to be pivotal. Hence Pound's reconstruction of the American Civil War as a plan of the usurocracy; all proved by two lines of a letter from one broker to another. The quotation is authentic I am sure but so what? Can it prove against all other evidence of the causes of the Civil War that it was planned by the usurocracy? Yes – if you are willing to believe it. For anyone not caught in the web of that thinking, it is obviously balderdash.

Pound's friends, William Carlos Williams, Hemingway, E. E. Cummings, all knew that what Pound was talking was balderdash and told him so. But his mind was made up. 'He was also isolated in the sense that he was imprisoned in a world of his own – a man with a mission to change the world both culturally and economically' (Stock, p. 371). Cummings told him he was 'Ikey-Ikey, Wandering Jew, Quo Vadis, Oppressed Minority of one, Misunderstood Master, Mister Lonelyheart, and Man Without a Country' (Torrey, p. 159).

Pound, however, went on claiming that he was a patriotic American: 'I consider myself a hundred per cent American and a patriot. I am only against Roosevelt and the Jews who influence him' (Torrey, p. 160).

There was, to be sure, a lot of anti-Roosevelt sentiment within America. The isolationists and the pro-German lobby did not want the USA to go to war. Roosevelt was criticized for leaning towards the British. To call Roosevelt names such as 'Jewsfelt', as Pound did, was not unique to him: the American, William Dudley Pelley, who founded the fascist organization Silver Legion (his followers known as Silver Shirts), called him 'Rosenfelt' (Schlesinger, p. 81). Pound joined the international anti-Semitic tendency as he signed up for the radio broadcasts. Now he could – indeed he had to – display more prominently the prejudices he had just polished up. This is why the pamphlets I have discussed in Chapter V – the Italian pamphlets – are much more virulent than his earlier pamphlets, covered in Chapter IV.

The tragedy of Ezra Pound is that in exiling himself from America he kept on inflicting a hurt on himself that never healed. Whatever the pain of rejection at his college might have done to him, howsoever undervalued he may have felt at college and university and then in his first job (from which he had been fired), he could have grown out of it. But he never managed to; he stayed a brash kid all his life. Londoners looked askance at him when he went around in those early days with one earring and colourful clothes (recall the Herbert Read quote in Chapter II). But they accepted him as an exotic American and he stayed awkward in his behaviour all his life as if refusing to grow up. Yet he craved for acceptance back home. He kept on helping Americans who joined him abroad, he went on writing for American magazines and little reviews. He bombarded their newspapers and dabbled in political comment. All the time it was as if he was saying, *Look at me. Look at me. Now. Do you think I am all right, acceptable, American?* But again and again the answer was not to his satisfaction.

So he upped the ante and finally committed an act of treason in which he saw himself as the most loyal American, the only one who could defend the Constitution against all comers. In persisting in broadcasting after Pearl Harbor he must have known – indeed there is evidence that he did – that he was overstepping the mark. His defence was that he was only against Roosevelt and his Jewish advisers not against America. This was super loyalty now become treason. The traitor is loyal to his own concept of his country, Lord Haw-Haw no less than Ezra Pound.

But he was caught no less in his vision of America than he was in his vision of Europe. As I argued earlier, his ideal American, Jefferson, was part of the European Enlightenment, a squire like any English squire but with lands across the Atlantic. He and John Adams and many of their circle came to Europe and felt at home. Pound was trained in that mould but by then he was one of a tiny minority of European-Enlightenment Americans. The reality of the Europe that arrived on Americans' doorsteps had little to do with Enlightenment – these were arrivals from the hidden underbelly of Europe, subject to anti-Semitic pogroms or driven from it by poverty. Pound avoided living with that Europe by going to its western, 'more civilized' parts – London and Paris. He would absorb Europe and take it back to America. He would be the new Jefferson who could converse in French and write with an intimate knowledge of Latin and Greek. So Pound fell in love with an eighteenth-century America and defined that as his cultural home. That is where he wanted his country to get back to. But there were obstacles. The demons that stood in the way were readily provided by the new perversions – or rather the resurgence of the old perversions – in Europe itself. European anti-Semitism and fascism, its Anti-Enlightenment ideologies were taken up by Pound for an explanation of why his old country could not be like its eighteenth-century squirearchical Republic again. It was the Jews, the usurocrats, the Rothschilds who stood in the way. Defeated Europe – Germany especially – had embraced that answer under

Hitler. Now with economic desolation across Europe that answer could be taken up by Major Douglas as well as Ezra Pound.

But Pound profoundly misunderstood what America was about, what his old country had become. The country he left in 1908 was rich but powerless on the world stage. Within a generation Britain had been displaced and America was jostling for leadership of the world. The Depression distracted everyone but Roosevelt, and his New Deal cemented America's liberal capitalism and made it a world leader after the Second World War. America overcame European dominance by going about its development in its own way, borrowing from Europe but also innovating along its own path.

America was no longer the western province of the Empire. America was the new Roman Empire.

Ezra Pound's life in self-imposed exile coincided with this transition of America from a periphery of the Empire to its metropolis. The Europe that Pound returned to after St Elizabeth's was a junior partner to America. Pound lived through a cultural revolution in America and missed it completely.

That was perhaps his greatest tragedy.

Select Bibliography

Ackroyd, Peter, *Ezra Pound and his World*, London: Thames & Hudson, 1980

Acres, W. Marston, *The Bank of England From Within 1694-1900*, two volumes, London: the Bank of England/Oxford University Press, 1931

Aquinas, St Thomas, *Political Writings* (ed. R. W. Dyson), Cambridge: Cambridge University Press, 2002

Aristotle, *The Politics* (trans. T. A. Sinclair; ed. Trevor Saunders), London: Penguin Books, 2002

Brooker, Peter, *A Student's Guide to the Selected Poems of Ezra Pound*, London: Faber and Faber, 1979

Brookhiser, Richard, *Alexander Hamilton, American*, New York: Free Press, 1999

Buchan, James, *Frozen Desire: An Inquiry into the Meaning of Money*, London: Picador, 1997

Cappon, Lester J. (ed.), *The Adams-Jefferson Letters: The Complete Correspondence between Thomas Jefferson and Abigail and John Adams*, two volumes, North Carolina: the University of North Carolina Press, 1959

Chick, Victoria, *On Money, Method and Keynes: Selected Essays* (ed. Philip Arestis and Sheila Dow), London: Macmillan, 1992

Clapham, John Sir, *The Bank of England: A History*, two volumes, Cambridge: Cambridge University Press, 1944

Clark, Martin, *Modern Italy, 1871-1995*, second edition, London: Longman, 1996

Cole, G. D. H., Colin Clark, Evan Frank Mottram Durbin (eds.), *What Everybody Wants to Know about Money: a planned outline of monetary problems*, London: Gollancz, 1933

Corry, Bernard Alexander, *Money, Saving and Investment in English Economics, 1800 to 1850*, London: Macmillan, 1962
Desai, Meghnad, *Marxian Economics*, Oxford: Basil Blackwell, 1979
– *Testing Monetarism*, London: Frances Pinter, 1981
– 'A Basic Income Proposal', 1998, in Robert Skidelsky, et al., *The State of the Future*, 1998
– *Marx's Revenge: The Resurgence of Capitalism and the Death of Statist Socialism*, London: Verso, 2002
– and Yahya Said, 'The New Anti-Capitalist Movement: Money and Global Civil Society' in Kaldor, Anheier and Glasius (eds.) *Global Civil Society Yearbook 2003*
Douglas, C. H., *Economic Democracy*, London: Cecil Palmer, 1920
– *Social Power and Democracy*, London: Cecil Palmer, 1921
Durbin, E. F. M., *Purchasing Power and Trade Depression: A Critique of Underconsumption Theories*, London: Jonathan Cape, 1933
Eatwell, John, et al. (eds.), *The New Palgrave Dictionary of Economics*, London: Palgrave Macmillan, 1998
Feldman, Gerald D., *The Great Disorder: Politics, Economics and Society in the German Inflation, 1914-24*, New York: Oxford University Press USA, 1993
Finlay, John, *Social Credit: The English Origins*, London and Montreal: McGill-Queen's University Press, 1972
Fletcher, George, *Our Secret Constitution: How Lincoln Redefined American Democracy*, New York: Oxford University Press USA, 2003
Friedman, M. and A. Schwartz, *A Monetary History of the United States 1867–1960*, Princeton NJ: Princeton University Press, 1963
Gaitskell, H. T. N., 'Four Monetary Heretics' in Cole, G. D. H., et al., *What Everybody Wants To Know About Money*, 1933
Galbraith John Kenneth, *Money: Whence It Came, Where It Went*, Boston, Mass.: Houghton Mifflin, 1975, 1996, 2001; London:

SELECT BIBLIOGRAPHY

Deutsch, 1975; Penguin Books, 1977, 1988, 1995
Goodwin, Craufurd D. (ed.), *Art and the Market: Roger Fry on Commerce in Art – Selected Writings*, Ann Arbor: University of Michigan Press, 1998
Hayek F. A., *Prices and Production*, London: Routledge, 1931
Hertz, Noreena, *IOU: The Debt Threat and Why We Must Defuse It*, London: Fourth Estate, 2004
Hollis, Christopher, *The Two Nations: A Financial Study of English History*, London: Routledge, 1935
Ingersoll, J. E., 'Interest Rates' (1987) in Eatwell, John, et al., *The New Palgrave Dictionary of Economics*, vol. 2
Jones, Howard Mumford, *Revolution and Romanticism*, Cambridge, Mass.: Harvard University Press, 1974
Judd, Alan, *Ford Madox Ford*, London: HarperCollins, 1990
Julius, Anthony, *T. S. Eliot, Anti-Semitism and Literary Form*, Cambridge: Cambridge University Press, 1995
Kaldor, Mary, Helmut Anheier and Marlies Glasius (eds.), *Global Civil Society Yearbook 2003*, London Centre for Civil Society and Centre for the Study of Global Governance, LSE, 2003
Kenner, Hugh, *The Pound Era*, Berkeley: University of California Press, 1973
Keynes, John Maynard, 'The Means to Prosperity' (1933), *The Collected Writings of John Maynard Keynes: Essays in Persuasion Vol. IX*, London: Palgrave Macmillan, 1985
– *The General Theory of Employment, Interest and Money*, London: Macmillan, 1936
Kindleberger, Charles, *The World in Depression 1929–1939*, Berkeley: University of California Press, 1986
Lester, Richard A., *Monetary Experiments: Early American and Recent Scandinavian*, Princeton, NJ: Princeton University Press, 1939; Newton Abbot: David & Charles, 1970
Lewis, Wyndham, *Blasting and Bombardiering*, London, Calder & Boyars, 1967

Martin, Wallace (ed.), *Orage as Critic*, London: Routledge, 1974

Materer, Timothy, *Vortex: Pound, Eliot and Lewis*, Ithaca: Cornell University Press, 1979

Mehrling, Perry, *Money Interest and Public Interest: American Monetary Thought 1920–1970*, Cambridge, Mass.: Harvard University Press, 1997

Monbiot, George, *The Age of Consent*, London: Flamingo, 2003

Morrison, Paul, *The Poetics of Fascism: Ezra Pound, T. S. Eliot, Paul De Man*, New York: Oxford University Press USA, 1996

Nicholls, Peter, *Ezra Pound: Politics, Economics and Writings –A Study of the Cantos*, London: Palgrave Macmillan, 1984

Noonan, John T., *The Scholastic Analysis of Usury*, Cambridge, Mass.: Harvard University Press, 1957

Overholser, Willis A., *A short review and analysis of the history of money in the United States: With an introduction to the current money problem*, New York: Progress Publishing Concern, 1936

Overy, Richard, *War and Economy in the Third Reich*, Oxford: Clarendon Press, 1994

Panico, Carlo, 'Interest and Profit' in Eatwell, John, et al., *The New Palgrave Dictionary of Economics*, 1998

Parry, Jonathan and Maurice Bloch (eds.), *Money and the Morality of Exchange*, Cambridge: Cambridge University Press, 1989

Pocock, J. G. A., *Virtue, Commerce, and History: Essays on Political Thought and History, Chiefly in the Eighteenth Century*, Cambridge: Cambridge University Press, 1985

Reck, Michael, *Ezra Pound: A Close-Up*, London: Hart-Davis, 1968

Said, Yahya, and Meghnad Desai, 'The New Anti-Capitalist Movement: Money and Global Civil Society' in Kaldor, Anheier and Glasius, *Global Civil Society Yearbook 2003*

Samuelson, Paul, 'An Exact Consumption Loan Model of Interest without the Social Contrivance of Money', *Journal of Political Economy*, December 1958, pp. 467–82

Sayle, Catherine, ed., *Charles Olson and EP: An Encounter at St.*

SELECT BIBLIOGRAPHY

Elizabeth's, London: Routledge, 1974

Schlesinger, Arthur M., *The Age of Roosevelt: 1935-1936 Vol 3: The Politics of Upheaval*, Boston, Mass.: Houghton-Mifflin, 1958, 2003

Skidelsky, Robert, *John Maynard Keynes Vol 2: The Economist as Saviour, 1920-37*, London: Macmillan, 1992

– *John Maynard Keynes Vol 3: Fighting for Britain, 1937-1946*, London: Macmillan, 2000

Skidelsky, Robert, Walter Eltis, Evan Davis, Norman Gemmell, Meghnad Desai, *The State of the Future*, London: Social Market Foundation, 1998

Spengler, Oswald, *The Decline of the West*, New York: Random House, 1945; Oxford University Press USA, 1991

Stock, Noel, *The Life of Ezra Pound*, New York: Pantheon Books, 1970; London: Random House, 1970

– (ed.), *Ezra Pound Perspective: Essays in Honor of His Eightieth Birthday*. Chicago: H. Regnery Co., 1965.

– (ed.), *Impact: Essays on Ignorance and the Decline of American Civilization*, Chicago: Henry Regnery, 1960

Torrey, E. Fuller, *The Roots of Treason: Ezra Pound and the Secret of St. Elizabeth's*, New York: McGraw Hill, 1984

Tytell, John, *Ezra Pound: The Solitary Volcano*, London: Anchor Books/Bloomsbury, 1987

Van Parijs, Philippe, *Real Freedom for All: What (If Anything) Can Justify Capitalism?*, Oxford: Clarendon Press, 1995

Zarlenga, Stephen A., *The Lost Science of Money: The Mythology of Money – The Story of Power*, New York: American Monetary Institute Charitable Trust, 2002

Index

A + B theorem, 82–4
Action, 134
Adams, Henry, 106–7
Adams, John, 123, 140
   'Jefferson–Adams Letters as a Shrine and a Monument, The' (Pound), 10–11, 106–7, 109, 111
Adams, John Quincy, 72
America
   artists' position in, 21, 52, 77
   Civil War, 73, 101–2, 120–1, 138
   and European culture, 25–6, 130–2, 140
   immigrants to America, 20–2, 24, 121, 140
   War of Independence (American Revolution), 71, 107, 121
American Review, 105, 134
American Revolution (War of American Independence), 71, 107, 121
anti-globalization, 16, 17, 133
anti-Semitism, 1, 2–3, 11n, 22, 116, 139
Aquinas, St Thomas, 56, 59–60, 61n
Aristotle, *Politics*, 52–3, 57
armaments manufacture, 38, 95
art and artists
   in America, 21, 52, 77
   and capitalist economy, 48–50
   commodification of art, 17, 47, 51–2
   and credit restriction, 78–9
   modernist movements, 26–7
   and patronage, 47–9, 101
Athenaeum, 33
Augustine, St, 59

Banco San Georgio, 100
Bank of England, 26, 67–70, 118–19, 129
Bank of the United States, 72, 120, 124–5
bankers and banking, 42–3, 56, 67–70, 92, 99–100
   see also Bank of England; Bank of the United States; central banking; Federal Reserve System
Banking Act 1844, 69
banking holiday, 42, 74, 97
Beerbohm, Max, 34
Belloc, Hilaire, 83, 105
biblical injunctions against usury, 53–4
Biddle, Nicholas, 18, 72–3
Blackshirt movement, 134
Blast, 7, 30, 33
Board of Trade, and colonial currency, 71, 120n
Bollingen-Library of Congress Award, 13
Brooker, Peter, *A Student's Guide to the Selected Poems of Ezra Pound*, 15
Bryan, William Jennings, 18, 25, 67, 74

Calvin, John, 41
capitalism, 17, 47–51, 48–50, 62–3
Carnegie Endowment for Peace, *Report on the Effects of the War*, 38
central banking, 67, 74, 119
  see also Bank of England; Bank of the United States; Federal Reserve System
Chesterton, G. K., 83, 105
Christianity
  and anti-Semitism, 2–3
  Jews' conversion to, 2
  and usury, 41, 53–4, 56–7
Churchill, Winston, 67
Citizen's Income, 89–90
Civil War, American, 73, 101–2, 120, 138
Collins, Seward, 105, 134
commodification of art, 17, 47, 51–2
consumption loans, 55, 63–4
Cookson, William, Pound's *Selected Prose*, 116
credit restriction, 70, 78–9, 84–5, 89–90, 121
Credit, Social *see* Social Credit
Cummings, E. E., 14, 122, 132, 138

debt, 90–1, 100, 108–10
deflation, 69, 74
Depression *see* Great Depression
depression, agricultural, 121
devaluation of currency, 45
Dial, 38
Doolittle, Hilda (H.D.), 4, 132
Douglas, C. H., 44, 95, 115
  A + B theorem, 82–4
  Economic Democracy, 33, 81
  Social Credit, 8, 33, 83–5, 137

Durbin, Evan, 84

effective demand, 83, 90, 137–8
Eliot, T. S., 1, 4, 122
employment levels, 32, 84, 96
  in America, 98
  in Britain, 39, 42, 97, 115
  in Germany, 99
English Review, 28
European culture, America and, 25–6, 130–2, 140
Exile, 36

Fascist economic policies, 43, 115
Fascist Quarterly, 134
Federal Reserve System, 74, 81, 98, 113
Finlay, John, *Social Credit: The English Origins*, 84, 137
First World War
  economic background to, 10–11, 38, 111
  and Vorticist movement, 7, 29–30
Fisher, Irvine, 99
Ford, Ford Madox (Ford Madox Hueffer), 27, 28, 34, 40, 134
Friedman, Milton, 94
Frost, Robert, 33
Fry, Roger, 'Art and Commerce', 48–50
full employment, 32, 42, 84, 96, 115

Gaitskell, Hugh, 44, 84n
Gaudier-Brzeska, Henri, 7, 30
General Strike, 39
George, Henry, 103–4
German economy, 42–3, 99, 104, 115
Gessell, Silvio, 40, 102–4, 134

INDEX

The Natural Economic Order, 103
gold, 16, 25, 73–4, 98
Gold Standard, 25, 31, 45, 79–80
    and unemployment in Britain, 39, 42, 97
Goodwin, Craufurd, *Art and the Market*, 49–50
Great Depression, 40, 74, 93–4, 103
greenbacks, 73, 121, 126
Griffiths, D. W., 2

Hamilton, Alexander, 18, 71–2, 93, 108, 123, 126
Haw-Haw, Lord (William Joyce), 12, 140
Hayek, F. A., *Prices and Production*, 84
Hemingway, Ernest, 12, 38, 39, 138
Hitler, Adolf, 42–3, 115
Hueffer, Ford Madox *see* Ford, Ford Madox
Hulme, T. E., 83
Hume, David, 93
hyperinflation, 31

Imagist movement, 28
immigrants to America, 20–1, 24, 121, 140
inflation, 73, 91, 93–4, 121
    hyperinflation, 31
interest and interest rates
    Aristotle on, 52–3, 57
    in Britain, 42, 97
    classical theories, 62, 65–6
    interest-free debt, 55, 90, 91, 109–10
    in Islamic banking, 61, 110–11
    and productivity, 63, 91–2
international debt, 19, 64–5, 133

International Economic Conference, 45
International Monetary Fund (IMF), 19, 133
Islamic injunctions against usury, 54, 61, 110–11
Italian economy, 43, 104–5, 115

Jackson, Andrew, 18, 41–2, 72, 102
James, Henry, 27
Jefferson, Thomas, 17, 72, 93, 123
    'Jefferson–Adams Letters as a Shrine and a Monument, The' (Pound), 10–11, 106–7, 109, 111
Jews and Judaism, 2, 11, 15, 23, 116
    injunctions against usury, 53–4, 56
    see also anti-Semitism
Joyce, James, 38
Joyce, William (Lord Haw-Haw), 12, 140
Judd, Alan, *Ford Madox Ford*, 34

Kant, Immanuel, 52
Kasper, John, 128–9
Keynes, J. M., 44, 65–6, 90, 94–7, 102–4
    The General Theory of Employment, Interest and Money, 45, 61–2, 83, 84
Kitson, Arthur, 41
Koran, injunctions against usury, 54

Lenin, Vladimir Ilyich, *Imperialism*, 32
Lewis, Wyndham, 4, 29–30
    Blast, 7
    'The Revolutionary Simpleton', 38

Lincoln, Abraham, 126
Little Review, 33
loans, 55, 63–4

Madison, James, 72
Marwood, Arthur, 'A Complete Actuarial Scheme for Insuring John Doe against all the Vicissitudes of Life', 28
Marx, Karl, 41, 58, 62–3
 anti-Marxian socialism, 104
 Economic and Philosophical Manuscripts, 47
 mass production, 51
Material Party, 96
Mazzini, Guiseppe, 121
Mediterranean civilization, pre-Renaissance, 41, 60, 107
Merchant of Venice, The (Shakespeare), 60–1
migration to America, 20–2, 24, 121, 140
minimum wage, 89
monetarism, 18, 94
money, 46–7, 58, 62–3, 65, 114–15
 in earlier societies, 51–2, 55, 60
 stamped money, 102–3
money supply, 90, 94, 129
Monroe, Harriet, 35
Morrison, Paul, *The Poetics of Fascism*, 15
mortgages, 63–4
Mosley, Oswald, 134
Mussolini, Benito, 9, 39–40, 43, 94, 104, 127

Nation, The, 36
National Debt, 69, 72
nationalism, 5–6, 26

Nazis, German economy under, 42–3, 115
New Age, 5, 29
New Deal, 77, 97–8, 105, 141
New English Weekly, 94
New Masses, 35
New York Herald, 33
Nicholls, Peter, *Ezra Pound: Politics, Economics and Writings*, 17
North American Review, 106

Olson, Charles, 30
Orage, A. R., 7–8, 28–9, 40, 83, 94
Overholser, Willis A., *A short review and analysis of the history of money in the United States*, 120

Paterson, William, 68, 118–19
patronage of the arts, 47–9, 101
Pelley, William Dudley, 139
Poetry, 35
Pound, Ezra
 family background, 24–5, 125
 personal appearance, 27, 28
 ABC of Economics, 79, 81, 86–96
 'America, Roosevelt and the Causes of the Present War', 125–7
 'Bureaucracy the Flail of Jehovah', 8, 36–7
 'Canto LXXIV', 11n
 'Canto LXXVIII', 122
 'Canto XLV', 56, 100, 101
 'For a New Paideuma', 9
 '*Gold and Work*', 123
 'Individual in his Milieu, The', 102–4
 'Introduction to the Economic

Nature of the United States, An', 123–4
'Jefferson–Adams Letters as a Shrine and a Monument, The', 10–11, 106–7, 109, 111
Money Pamphlets by £, 40, 77
'Murder by Capital', 9, 78–9
'National Culture – A Manifesto', 112–13
'Passport Nuisance, The', 36
Patria Mia, 5, 20–2
Pisan Cantos, 13, 117, 122
'Provincialism the Enemy', 5–6, 7
'Social Credit: An Impact', 97, 99, 101–2
'State, The', 35
Visiting Card, A, 117–22
'What is Money For?', 114–16
Pound, Homer Loomis, 24, 25, 125
Pound, Isabel Weston, 24
Pound, Thaddeus, 24, 125
pre-Renaissance civilization, Mediterranean, 41, 60, 107

radio broadcasts, Pound's wartime, 11–12, 15, 139
Read, Herbert, 27, 83
religion, Pound's attacks on, 40–1
Report on the Effects of the War (Carnegie Endowment for Peace), 38
Revolution, American (War of American Independence), 71, 107, 121
riba, 61, 111
Ricardo, David, 62
Riefensthal, Leni, 2
risk, 59, 61, 62

'Robber Barons', 25
Roosevelt, Franklin D., 42, 74, 127, 135
  anti-Roosevelt sentiment, 23, 105–6, 139
Russell, Bertrand, 29
Russell, Peter, 40, 77, 117

Samuelson, Paul Anthony, 66
Schacht, Hjalmar, 99, 104
Schlesinger, Arthur, *The Age of Roosevelt*, 105n
Seeward, William Henry, 126–7
Shakespear, Dorothy, 6, 28
Shakespear, Olivia, 28
Shakespeare, William, *The Merchant of Venice*, 60–1
Shaw, G. B., 14n, 29
  Heartbreak House, 19
Shays' Rebellion, 71
silver, 25, 73–4, 98
Silver Legion/Silver Shirts, 139
Social Credit, 33, 83, 84–5, 137–8
  Pound's support for, 8, 11, 22, 77, 105, 122
Socialism, 26, 29, 32, 104
Socialist International, 26
Spengler, Oswald, *The Decline of the West*, 32
stamped money, 102–3
Stock, Noel
  Impact: Essays on Ignorance and the Decline of American Civilization, 112
  The Life of Ezra Pound, 27, 135–6

Tagore, Rabindranath, 27
taxation, 19, 95, 107–8
Tobin, James, 19

Torrey, E. Fuller, *The Roots of Treason: Ezra Pound and the Secret of St Elizabeth's*, 135
treason, Pound's indictment for, 12, 15

unemployment *see* employment levels
usurocracy, and decline of American culture, 112, 119
usury, 14, 101, 103, 116, 118, 122–5
    religious and philosophical injunctions against, 16, 41, 53–7, 59, 61
utopian economics, 89

Van Buren, Martin, 18, 41, 73, 89, 102, 124–5
Vidal, Gore, 102
Vorticist movement, 7, 28, 33

wages, minimum, 89
Walpole, Robert, 69, 108
war, economic causes of, 38, 111, 118, 125
War of American Independence (American Revolution), 71, 107, 121
Warhol, Andy, 51
Webb, Beatrice, *The Decay of Capitalism*, 32
Weston, Frances (Frank), 25
William of Auxerre, 59–60
Williams, William Carlos, 12, 113, 132, 134, 138
work certificates, 86, 88–9
working hours, 80, 87, 93

Yeats, W. B., 6, 27